Memories in Focus

THE AZRIELI SERIES OF HOLOCAUST SURVIVOR MEMOIRS: PUBLISHED TITLES

ENGLISH TITLES

Judy Abrams, *Tenuous Threads/* Eva Felsenburg Marx, *One of the Lucky Ones*

Amek Adler, *Six Lost Years*

Molly Applebaum, *Buried Words*

Claire Baum, *The Hidden Package*

Bronia and Joseph Beker, *Joy Runs Deeper*

Tibor Benyovits, *Unsung Heroes*

Max Bornstein, *If Home Is Not Here*

Felicia Carmelly, *Across the Rivers of Memory*

Tommy Dick, *Getting Out Alive*

Marian Domanski, *Fleeing from the Hunter*

Anita Ekstein, *Always Remember Who You Are*

John Freund, *Spring's End*

Susan Garfield, *Too Many Goodbyes: The Diaries of Susan Garfield*

Myrna Goldenberg (Editor), *Before All Memory Is Lost: Women's Voices from the Holocaust*

René Goldman, *A Childhood Adrift*

Elly Gotz, *Flights of Spirit*

Ibolya Grossman and Andy Réti, *Stronger Together*

Pinchas Gutter, *Memories in Focus*

Anna Molnár Hegedűs, *As the Lilacs Bloomed*

Rabbi Pinchas Hirschprung, *The Vale of Tears*

Bronia Jablon, *A Part of Me*

Helena Jockel, *We Sang in Hushed Voices*

Eddie Klein, *Inside the Walls*

Michael Kutz, *If, By Miracle*

Ferenc Laczó (Editor), *Confronting Devastation: Memoirs of Holocaust Survivors from Hungary*

Nate Leipciger, *The Weight of Freedom*

Alex Levin, *Under the Yellow and Red Stars*

Fred Mann, *A Drastic Turn of Destiny*

Michael Mason, *A Name Unbroken*

Leslie Meisels with Eva Meisels, *Suddenly the Shadow Fell*

Leslie Mezei, *A Tapestry of Survival*

Muguette Myers, *Where Courage Lives*

David Newman, *Hope's Reprise*

Arthur Ney, *W Hour*

Felix Opatowski, *Gatehouse to Hell*

Marguerite Élias Quddus, *In Hiding*

Maya Rakitova, *Behind the Red Curtain*

Henia Reinhartz, *Bits and Pieces*

Betty Rich, *Little Girl Lost*

Paul-Henri Rips, *E/96: Fate Undecided*

Margrit Rosenberg Stenge, *Silent Refuge*

Steve Rotschild, *Traces of What Was*

Judith Rubinstein, *Dignity Endures*

Martha Salcudean, *In Search of Light*

Kitty Salsberg and Ellen Foster, *Never Far Apart*

Joseph Schwarzberg, *Dangerous Measures*

Zuzana Sermer, *Survival Kit*

Rachel Shtibel, *The Violin/* Adam Shtibel, *A Child's Testimony*

Maxwell Smart, *Chaos to Canvas*

Gerta Solan, *My Heart Is At Ease*

Zsuzsanna Fischer Spiro, *In Fragile Moments/* Eva Shainblum, *The Last Time*

George Stern, *Vanished Boyhood*

Willie Sterner, *The Shadows Behind Me*

Ann Szedlecki, *Album of My Life*

William Tannenzapf, *Memories from the Abyss/* Renate Krakauer, *But I Had a Happy Childhood*

Elsa Thon, *If Only It Were Fiction*

Agnes Tomasov, *From Generation to Generation*

Joseph Tomasov, *From Loss to Liberation*

Sam Weisberg, *Carry the Torch/* Johnny Jablon, *A Lasting Legacy*

Leslie Vertes, *Alone in the Storm*

Anka Voticky, *Knocking on Every Door*

Memories in Focus
Pinchas Gutter

WITH THE ASSISTANCE OF MYRNA RIBACK,
AS PART OF THE AZRIELI FOUNDATION'S
SUSTAINING MEMORIES PROGRAM

THE AZRIELI FOUNDATION
www.azrielifoundation.org

Cover and book design by Mark Goldstein.
Cover image courtesy of USC Shoah Foundation — Institute for Visual History and Education
Endpaper maps by Martin Gilbert
Map on page xxv by François Blanc

LIBRARY AND ARCHIVES CANADA CATALOGUING IN PUBLICATION

Gutter, Pinchas, 1932– , author
    Memories in Focus/ Pinchas Gutter; with the assistance of Myrna Riback, as part of the Azrieli Foundation's Sustaining Memories Program.

(Azrieli series of Holocaust survivor memoirs. Series IX)
Includes bibliographical references and index.
ISBN 978-1-988065-24-3 (softcover)

1. Gutter, Pinchas, 1932–. 2. Holocaust, Jewish (1939–1945) — Poland — Personal narratives. 3. Jewish children in the Holocaust — Poland — Biography. 4. Holocaust survivors — Canada — Biography. 5. Autobiographies. I. Azrieli Foundation, issuing body II. Title. III. Series: Azrieli series of Holocaust survivor memoirs. Series IX

D804.48.G88 2017   940.53'18083   C2017-907842-9

PRINTED IN CANADA

The Azrieli Series of Holocaust Survivor Memoirs

Naomi Azrieli, Publisher

Jody Spiegel, Program Director
Arielle Berger, Managing Editor
Matt Carrington, Editor
Devora Levin, Assistant Editor
Elizabeth Lasserre, Senior Editor, French-Language Editions
Elin Beaumont, Community and Education Initiatives
Catherine Person, Education and Academic Initiatives/French Editor
Stephanie Corazza, Academic and Education Initiatives
Marc-Olivier Cloutier, School and Education Initiatives
Elizabeth Banks, Digital Asset Curator and Archivist
Catherine Quintal, Digital Communications Assistant

Mark Goldstein, Art Director
François Blanc, Cartographer
Bruno Paradis, Layout, French-Language Editions

Contents

Series Preface:
In their own words...

In telling these stories, the writers have liberated themselves. For so many years we did not speak about it, even when we became free people living in a free society. Now, when at last we are writing about what happened to us in this dark period of history, knowing that our stories will be read and live on, it is possible for us to feel truly free. These unique historical documents put a face on what was lost, and allow readers to grasp the enormity of what happened to six million Jews — one story at a time.

David J. Azrieli, C.M., C.Q., M.Arch
Holocaust survivor and founder, The Azrieli Foundation

Since the end of World War II, approximately 40,000 Jewish Holocaust survivors have immigrated to Canada. Who they are, where they came from, what they experienced and how they built new lives for themselves and their families are important parts of our Canadian heritage. The Azrieli Foundation's Holocaust Survivor Memoirs Program was established in 2005 to preserve and share the memoirs written by those who survived the twentieth-century Nazi genocide of the Jews of Europe and later made their way to Canada. The memoirs encourage readers to engage thoughtfully and critically with the complexities of the Holocaust and to create meaningful connections with the lives of survivors.

Millions of individual stories are lost to us forever. By preserving the stories written by survivors and making them widely available to a broad audience, the Azrieli Foundation's Holocaust Survivor Memoirs Program seeks to sustain the memory of all those who perished at the hands of hatred, abetted by indifference and apathy. The personal accounts of those who survived against all odds are as different as the people who wrote them, but all demonstrate the courage, strength, wit and luck that it took to prevail and survive in such terrible adversity. The memoirs are also moving tributes to people — strangers and friends — who risked their lives to help others, and who, through acts of kindness and decency in the darkest of moments, frequently helped the persecuted maintain faith in humanity and courage to endure. These accounts offer inspiration to all, as does the survivors' desire to share their experiences so that new generations can learn from them.

In 2011, the Azrieli Foundation, in partnership with Ryerson University in Toronto, created a new program called Sustaining Memories, designed to assist Holocaust survivors in writing their memoirs. From 2011–2018, the Sustaining Memories program trained adult or mature volunteers to work with Holocaust survivors to record their stories and assist them in producing a written manuscript for their families.

The Holocaust Survivor Memoirs Program collects, archives and publishes select survivor memoirs and makes the print editions available free of charge to educational institutions and Holocaust-education programs across Canada. They are also available for sale online to the general public. All revenues to the Azrieli Foundation from the sales of the Azrieli Series of Holocaust Survivor Memoirs go toward the publishing and educational work of the memoirs program.

~

The Azrieli Foundation would like to express appreciation to the following people for their invaluable efforts in producing this book: Doris Bergen, Mark Duffus (Maracle Inc), Barbara Kamieński, Farla Klaiman, Vivian Felsen, Therese Parent, Myrna Riback, Stephen Smith, and Margie Wolfe & Emma Rodgers of Second Story Press.

About the Glossary

The following memoir contains a number of terms, concepts and historical references that may be unfamiliar to the reader. For information on major organizations; significant historical events and people; geographical locations; religious and cultural terms; and foreign-language words and expressions that will help give context and background to the events described in the text, please see the glossary beginning on page 115.

Introduction

There was something special about my meeting with Pinchas Gutter that is hard to put into words. It was not that he was a Holocaust survivor, because when I met him I had already met hundreds of people who had survived the Holocaust. It was not that he was an amazing storyteller, even though I was mesmerized by his gentle tone and lyrical style. It was not that we shared an interest in music and had both lived in England, or that I had spent my childhood vacations in the Lake District of England, at the very place he was brought to as an orphan survivor. I am sure these shared qualities helped form a bond, but it was something to do with his *neshama*, his spirit, that was unusually captivating. He was both gentle and deep, and I felt like I could listen to him for hours. Little did I know that one day I would.

This book captures the story of Pinchas Gutter in his own words. You will witness the world of the Jews of Lodz, Poland, through the eyes of a five-year-old; the world of the Nazis through the eyes of a seven-year-old; the world of the Warsaw ghetto through the eyes of a ten-year-old; Majdanek concentration camp through the eyes of an eleven-year-old; slave labour through the eyes of a twelve-year-old; and finally, liberation through the eyes of a thirteen-year-old. You will observe the power of memory, and the ability to recall and retell the story of that boy as remembered by an eighty-five-year-old man.

Pinchas Gutter has told his story in many different ways over a twenty-year period. In 1993, he spoke on camera at Toronto's

Holocaust Memorial Centre and gave a four-hour interview about his life. In 1995, he gave another video interview to USC Shoah Foundation covering his life history. In 2002, I had the opportunity to make a documentary with him called *The Void: In Search of Memory Lost*, which was about his first visit back to Poland fifty-seven years after he was forced to leave the country after becoming a slave labourer. In 2014, he made another documentary, *Politische. Pole-Jude*, which tells his life story through visiting the places where he once lived. In 2015, he answered 1,500 questions about his life to become the first-ever interactive interviewee as a part of USC Shoah Foundation's New Dimensions in Testimony program. In 2017, he became the first Holocaust survivor to tell his story in full room-scale Virtual Reality. The VR piece "The Last Goodbye" allows viewers to join him as he journeys back to the Nazi death camp, Majdanek, and explains where he lived, including where his family was murdered.

In addition to telling his story in these various media formats, Pinchas lectures widely, attends and leads commemorations, speaks at Holocaust centres in Toronto, Cape Town, Johannesburg and other cities around the world and is a regular guest on the annual March of Remembrance and Hope, where each year he accompanies Canadian students to Poland and Germany. Over the years, as Pinchas relayed his testimony, I had the privilege of being his friend throughout the process, documenting the way in which his memory unfolded, listening for many hours to the details about his story.

My role in introducing this volume is not to tell the story of Pinchas Gutter for you but to reflect briefly on some themes to consider, which are deeply embedded in his story. There are many personal accounts about the Holocaust and all of them are different. No single experience was typical. People started in different places, came from different backgrounds, spoke different languages and had different ways of making decisions. The Nazis created a labyrinth of ghettos and camps that included rules and regulations that changed by the day — one SS officer was more brutal, another more cunning.

If someone had relatives or knew gentiles, these connections could make all the difference. A variety of factors meant that two family members starting in the same place with the same background could have completely different experiences based on luck and circumstance. The role of memory also comes into play, and how each person remembers details differently. A person's age and gender would also result in different narratives of the same events.

When you read the story of Pinchas Gutter, you will be reading an absolutely unique account of the Holocaust. While his account contains key historical facts and particular details that are relevant to other survivors, it is important to keep in mind that each survivor experienced these facts differently. Pinchas is no exception. His account brings both private and public memories to light in a way that is particular to his experience. There are a few key themes that stand out in his story: family, religion, resistance, morality, memory, loss and recovery.

Pinchas Gutter focuses on family for several reasons. The first is that as a child he had a vivid memory; even from infancy, Pinchas recalls details of family life. He remembers his father's daily routine, activities his mother carried out in the kitchen, his paternal grandfather's presence in his life, a fleeting memory of his paternal grandmother's death, and the farm where his maternal grandparents lived and worked. Pinchas has a sense of belonging and rootedness in Poland. Family represents security, love and heritage, which also extends to his aunts, uncles and cousins. He avoids pure nostalgia and at times relives the emotions and life they once lived. It is worth remembering that none of the people that he mentions — with the exception of his grandmother who died long before the war — has a grave he can visit. The inclusion of their names and the painting of the characters is in itself an act of memorial, which is particularly true for his twin sister, Sabina. The loss of his twin is like losing a part of himself. When he writes about her, he gives back a part of her life and creates a lasting memorial to her.

In terms of religion, Pinchas was brought up in a Hasidic household, which meant strict observance of Jewish laws and Hasidic customs. His descriptions of his daily life as a child bear out the routines and the sense of loyalty to the Torah and to the leaders of the community to which his family belonged, especially the Gerrer Rebbe, who was the chief rabbi of their sect. Pinchas uses terminology that belongs to his faith tradition or that references specific parts of the Yiddish culture from which he comes. Yiddish, the language used by East European Jews, has a deeply rooted relationship between language and culture that is not easily translated. He uses these terms in their original form to help explain the Jewish milieu in which he lived, and still does to this day. He is careful to show how the arrival of the Nazis and the imposition of their laws made it extremely difficult to survive as a practising Jew. He recounts experiences that illustrate the difficulties of inhabiting a Jewish identity, such as his refusal as a young boy to have his *peyes* (the sidelocks of hair worn by Hasidic men) cut off, even when his parents, who were observant Jews, insisted that he do so. He also discusses how the everyday religious practices his family followed before the Nazi period became increasingly difficult to observe in a meaningful way. The more restrictions the Nazis imposed, the less possible it was to practise. He gives glimpses of his family's struggle to maintain their religious identity as the Nazis removed one basic right after another.

Pinchas's testimony exemplifies various modes of resistance. On the one hand, the Gutters' family life was stripped away, and it appears that Pinchas's parents quickly decided to conceal their religion as a survival technique. On the other hand, there are repeated insights into the family's prayer practice, and how Pinchas's parents attempted to maintain a Jewish education for their son. This act of defiance is often referred to as spiritual resistance — maintaining one's religious and spiritual identity even when the system in power is structured to destroy it. In 1942, when Pinchas's father, Mendel, prays secretly with his son in an attic on Yom Kippur, the act not only is a defiant one but also plays a defining role in Pinchas's identity. The fact that Mendel had the strength to perform this meaningful act with his son provides an enduring sense of strength for Pinchas who, to this day, leads the Yom Kippur services at the Kiever Synagogue in Toronto. Similarly, Pinchas recalls the experience of having his bar mitzvah in the Częstochowa slave labour camp, when Rabbi Godel Eisner gathered together a *minyan* of ten Jewish men and — against the rules of the camp, which forbade collective worship — blessed the then thirteen-year-old Pinchas. This act was a defining moment both of his experience in the camp and in his development as a Jewish man. Resistance is also present in his story through the small acts of his parents to keep him and his twin sister, Sabina, alive. The family lived through the Warsaw Ghetto Uprising, in which Pinchas's observations vividly detail the armed resistance and how his family were, briefly, not victims but armed combatants against their foes. The sight of the twelve-year-old twins with their hands up in surrender was not because they were victims but because, momentarily, they were being feared.

In terms of the theme of morality, there is no sense that Pinchas views the world as a black-and-white divide between evil Nazi perpetrators and innocent Jewish victims. From a moral perspective, even under such an extreme situation in which independent choices were more difficult to make, he reveals that people did make choices and had to live by them. There were only very rare occasions when he encountered German guards in a personal way, and only one *Oberscharführer* — senior sergeant — who was even remotely helpful. Pinchas is quick to acknowledge how that official's personal gesture of placing him in the kitchen helped him, but also understands that the motive was not one of compassion. The *Oberscharführer* asks Pinchas to steal food from the kitchen in return for him being placed there to work. The transaction probably saved Pinchas's life, as he gets much-needed nourishment at a critical point, but he cannot thank the guard for his generosity of spirit because even in that situation, Pinchas was merely an instrument of the guard's will. It is his regrettable experience, and therefore conclusion, that in the world of murderous oppression created by the Nazis, there was no room for human compassion toward the Jews. Pinchas was closer to his fellow Jews and therefore is able to provide a more intimate perspective of the choices that Jews made. We learn of Jews who had a chance to use the relative privilege they had secured for good, like the Jewish policeman, Katz, who helped Pinchas in the work camp at Skarżysko. In the same work camp, we also hear of Fela Markowiczowa, the Jewish women's work commandant, whom he describes as "not a nice woman." Of course, he understates the power she wielded over the Jews in her control in return for her own protection and that of her family. He wants his readers to know that the choices were complex and that not all victims were victims in the same way.

Memory is probably the most prominent theme throughout Pinchas's story, although at times it is a little more difficult to detect. There is a sense that he is not only *telling* his story but *re-living* it. He carefully re-constructs his home and family life, takes us into the kitchen, allows us to *feel* his family, *feel* the freedom of being in the mountains when he was sick; he wants us to *feel* a visceral sense of physical pain and personal disappointment when he describes being attacked outside a church. There is a misperception that historical autobiographies, like this one, are designed as factual accounts. The episodes described all happen, but the details we remember and the importance we assign to them are not because of the facts themselves but how those events made us feel at the time. This is particularly true of extreme events, which have a tendency to remain more vivid due to the strong emotions associated with them. Reading Pinchas's memoir, it is worth asking why he might have chosen particular episodes that stand out and what the emotion is behind those memories. For example, he describes asking a man with boils where his father had gone, immediately after the selection in Majdanek. The specificity with which he writes, "He didn't say a word, he just lifted his head to heaven," clearly shows that Pinchas has a deep sense of how he felt in that moment, in that the man's unforgettable gesture becomes ingrained in his memory for the rest of his life.

No memory is more painful than the loss of his twin sister, Sabina. The closeness of his relationship with her and being children together, at eleven years old, intensifies the cruel manner of her death. The details of this experience give insight into the guilt and despair he still feels over her murder. But it is not the physical loss of Sabina that stands out most — it is the ultimate loss of her memory that weighs most heavily on Pinchas. As her twin, he was close to her, but somehow the memory of what she was like as a child, who she was as a person, how her face looked, all elude his memory. This inability to remember is particularly stark because he makes clear in other parts of his story just how good his visual memory is. The loss of Sabina is therefore a double blow. She is the one he wants to remember the most, yet he cannot retrieve her. Ironically, the depth of that loss is what drives him to recall and tell his story because he not only voices the story for himself, but every time he does so, including in this book, he retrieves Sabina from the ultimate loss of being forgotten altogether.

As painful as the loss of Sabina was, Pinchas's recovery of memories helps provide some hope to his otherwise soul-destroying experience. No more so than the rediscovery of his camp friend, Yaakov. In 2002, I was with Pinchas and his wife, Dorothy, in Poland, making the documentary *The Void: In Search of Memory Lost*. It was his first trip back to Warsaw and he had arranged to meet Holocaust survivor Jakob Gutenbaum, who had been in the work camp Skarżysko-Kamienna with him. I sat in the room with the two of them as they discussed their pasts and was filming when Pinchas realized that the man he was sitting with was Yaakov, the boy he thought had been murdered fifty-five years earlier. I had heard Pinchas's story about how a young boy with a limp at Skarżysko-Kamienna had been pulled out of line right next to him. Only as both men talked was it revealed that Gutenbaum had actually managed to escape death and was transferred to a different camp, Schlieben, the following day. In that moment, not only was memory recovered but healing also took place. Prior to this meeting, the lack of closure meant that Pinchas had borne the loss of Yaakov as his only witness for over half a century. It is interesting to note that Pinchas saves the story of the meeting with Gutenbaum until the epilogue.

Memories in Focus is mostly about closure. There are many layers to the narrative, which are worth spending time to discover. It is an intricately woven tapestry of memory, facts, social history, religious perspectives and commentary on the meaning of the events. Each of the episodes that Pinchas is prepared to reveal to us have imbued in them many dimensions, which are not discernible up close. Like any tapestry, the individual stitches are intricately woven but only truly make sense when one stands back and views the entire piece as a whole. In this book, Pinchas stitches together the moments of his story that matter the most to him, each story chosen for its personal significance and universal relevance. He tells this story in order to no longer be alone in bearing its burden; he tells this story so that its readers can widen the circle, carry the memory and be the legacy that Sabina never had.

Stephen Smith
Finci Viterbi Executive Director,
USC Shoah Foundation — Institute for Visual History and Education
2017

RECOMMENDED READINGS

Langer, Lawrence L. *Holocaust Testimonies: The Ruins of Memory*. (New Haven: Yale University Press, 1993).

Shandler, Jeffrey. *Holocaust Memory in the Digital Age: Survivors' Stories and New Media Practices*. (Palo Alto: Stanford University Press, 2017).

Shenker, Noah. *Reframing Holocaust Testimony*. (Bloomington: Indiana University Press, 2015).

Smith, Stephen. *Making Memory: Creating Britain's First Holocaust Centre*, 2nd rev. ed. (Laxton: Quill Press, 2002).

Smith, Stephen. "What will we do when the survivors are gone?" *Holocaust Education: Challenges for the Future*. Eds. Carol Rittner and Tara Ronda. (Greensburg: National Catholic Center for Holocaust Education, Seton Hill University, 2014).

Spielberg, Stephen, and the Shoah Foundation. *Testimony: The Legacy of Schindler's List and the USC Shoah Foundation*. (HarperCollins, 2014).

Traum, David, Andrew Jones, Kia Hays, Heather Maio, Oleg Alexander, Ron Artstein, Paul Debevec et al. "New Dimensions in Testimony: Digitally preserving a Holocaust survivor's interactive storytelling." In *International Conference on Interactive Digital Storytelling*, pp. 269-281. Cham Springer, 2015.

USC Shoah Foundation Visual History Archive, Pinchas Gutter, 12 January, 1995, Interview Code 534.

FURTHER READINGS ON NEW DIMENSIONS IN TESTIMONY

http://abc7chicago.com/education/technology-tells-survivors-stories-at-illinois-holocaust-museum/1938500/
ABC: Technology tells survivors' stories at Illinois Holocaust Museum (4.30.17)

http://www.chicagotribune.com/entertainment/museums/ct-illinois-holocaust-museum-3d-survivor-stories-ent-0428-20160426-column.html
Chicago Tribune: Holocaust Museum, new 3-D technology bring survivor stories to life (4.27.16)

http://forward.com/life/tech/382220/keeping-holocaust-survivor-testimonies-alive-through-holograms/
Forward: Keeping Holocaust Survivor Testimonies Alive — Through Holograms (9.8.17)

https://www.theguardian.com/technology/2016/jun/18/holocaust-survivor-hologram-pinchas-gutter-new-dimensions-history
The Guardian: The virtual Holocaust survivor: how history gained new dimensions (6.18.16)

https://www.thejc.com/lifestyle/features/holocaust-memorial-day-who-will-teach-them-when-we-are-gone-1.58500
The Jewish Chronicle: Holocaust Memorial Day: Who will teach them when we are gone? (1.29.16)

http://jewishjournal.com/culture/lifestyle/175534/
Jewish Journal: Interacting with a 'virtual' Holocaust survivor (7.2.15)

http://money.cnn.com/2017/04/24/technology/shoah-foundation-holocaust-remembrance-day/index.html
CNN: Shoah Foundation is using technology to preserve Holocaust survivor stories (4.24.17)

https://motherboard.vice.com/en_us/article/kb733e/vr-sheffield-doc-fest-talk-to-refugees-and-holocaust-survivors
Motherboard/Vice: These VR Films Let Viewers Talk to Refugees and Holocaust Survivors. (6.17.16)

https://motherboard.vice.com/en_us/article/ez3m4p/in-the-future-the-holo-caust-is-just-another-hologram
Motherboard/Vice: In the Future, the Holocaust Is Just Another Hologram (4.25.17)

https://www.nytimes.com/2017/09/19/opinion/the-remembering-machine.html?r=0
New York Times: The Remembering Machine (9.19.17)

https://www.pcmag.com/article/343452/how-natural-language-tech-holograms-are-preserving-holocaus
PC Magazine: How Natural Language Tech, Holograms Are Preserving Holocaust Testimony

http://www.techzone360.com/topics/techzone/articles/2017/04/28/431620-what-if-could-speak-a-holocaust-survivor-now.htm
Tech Zone: What If You Could Speak to a Holocaust Survivor? Now You Can (4.28.17)

http://wgntv.com/2015/09/16/learn-the-lives-of-holocaust-survivors-through-innovative-new-technology/
WGN-TV- Chicago: Learn the lives of Holocaust survivors through innovative new technology (9.16.15)

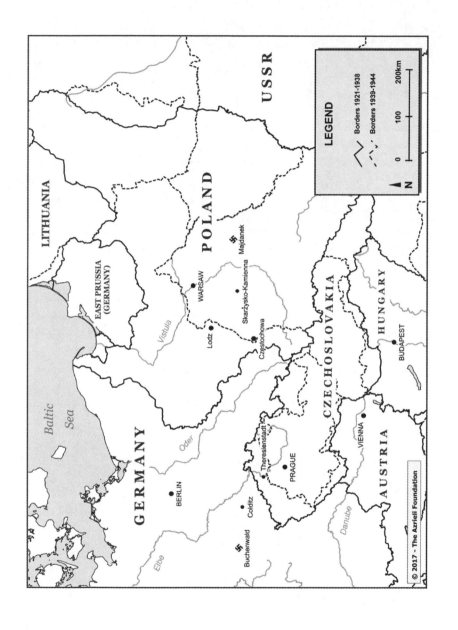

LEGEND

Borders 1921-1938
Borders 1939-1944

0   100   200km

N

LITHUANIA

USSR

POLAND

EAST PRUSSIA
(GERMANY)

Baltic
Sea

GERMANY

Vistula

WARSAW

Skarżysko-Kamienna

Majdanek

Lodz

Czestochowa

Oder

BERLIN

Elbe

Buchenwald

Colditz

Theresienstadt

PRAGUE

CZECHOSLOVAKIA

Danube

VIENNA

AUSTRIA

HUNGARY

BUDAPEST

© 2017 – The Azrieli Foundation

To my wife, Dorothy, my three children, Tanya, Jan and Rumi, my daughter-in-law, Lauren, and my grandchildren, Daniel, Adam and Lara.

Author's Preface

I am writing this book and publishing it specifically with the Azrieli Foundation because I think it is important that it end up in the right place. The Azrieli Foundation distributes its books to schools, and I strongly believe in the education of the young. In addition, the Foundation distributes these books free of charge. The memoirs are read and taught in schools and that gives people an opportunity to visualize what happened to us survivors and what can happen to anyone, because genocide is happening all the time. At this very moment, refugees from Syria, Africa, Afghanistan and Iraq are flooding into other countries because of the unspeakable lives they are forced to live in their own countries; for me specifically, it is heartbreaking to watch. When I see people, children, trudging along with their bundles, looking for hope of a better life, it hurts me. I've gone through that and I know what it is all about.

My purpose for writing this book is to show the pathos of my life — that of a boy who finds himself, at the young age of eight, in a maelstrom of iniquity and then somehow manages to live through that and goes on to build a life afterwards out of the ashes of that horror. I want to convey that there is more than the horror, that there is hope and that the world is not all bad. There is some good in the world. Even having gone through horrendous trauma, after suffering post-traumatic stress and having depressions and nightmares, there is the possibility of still leading a reasonably decent life. In spite of it all, there are parts of this life that you can still enjoy, maybe not as much as someone who didn't go through what you have, but still, you can have a life. Even more importantly, perhaps, you can go out and tell people what actually happened and try, bit by bit, to create a world that is a little better than the one you have known.

All I want is to impart a true picture, construct a tapestry of what has already happened, what can happen again and what shouldn't happen, if possible. I want to offer some kind of hope to people who are suffering injustice and tell them that one can outlive the evil and build a new life.

Pinchas Israel Gutter
2017

My First Life

I was born in Lodz, Poland, into a loving, middle-class family. We were a religious, Hasidic family who were not only followers of the Gerrer Rebbe but also very close to him.[1] He was magnificent looking, with a long white beard and clear eyes. His followers looked upon him as a sort of holy prince, and as he sat on a throne-like chair against the wall of his study, people would come to him with supplications and requests, hoping that he would intercede with God on their behalf.

My father's family were winemakers going back generations and we were, for 1930s Europe, considered quite well off. Each of my parents had a large extended family — two sets of grandparents and lots of uncles and aunts and cousins — but my immediate family was small, as my parents had only two children, my twin sister, Sabina, and me. We were born on July 21, 1932, and regrettably, or maybe luckily given what happened later, my mother had a very difficult childbirth and couldn't have any more children after we were born. So there were just the four of us. Even though I was only eleven years

---

1 For information on the Gerrer Rebbe as well as on other religious, historical and cultural terms; significant historical events and people; geographical locations; major organizations; and foreign-language words and expressions contained in the text, please see the glossary.

old when I lost almost my entire family, I remember them and the life we lived before the war extremely well. It is both fortunate and unfortunate to have such a vivid memory.

My family lived at ulica (street) Zachodnia 54, a four- or five-storey building right in the centre of town in a predominantly Jewish area. I know for sure that my family owned the building we lived in because I've got documents from the deeds office in Lodz that prove it. Zachodnia 54 was a typical Polish apartment block: a complex of four buildings surrounding a square inner courtyard. My paternal grandfather Yitzhak (or as he was called, Itche) Meir Gutter and his second wife lived in a small apartment next to ours and there was an adjoining door between the two apartments. My grandfather was a learned man, and as a philanthropist, he was the voluntary head of a charitable yeshiva, or seminary, where people were taught to be rabbis. In Poland, as in all of Eastern Europe at that time, it was common for Hasidim to create schools.

My grandfather was quite well known in Lodz. I have been told that, if you got off the train at the station in Lodz and asked where Itche Meir Gutter lived, any Jew on the street could tell you exactly that. He was that renowned.

My paternal grandparents had thirteen children but only five of them, three daughters and two sons, survived the influenza epidemic of 1918–1919. My paternal grandmother, Taube Tzeril Gutter, died in 1933, about a year after I was born, so I don't remember her, and my grandfather, in keeping with tradition, remarried after her death. We called his second wife *Ciocia Babcia*, which means Auntie Granny, and she was a very nice woman. My sister, Sabina, and I would often go over to visit my grandfather when we were small and I clearly remember that, in his bedroom on a stand opposite his bed, he had a metal chest, a kind of huge strong box, which was gilded and fashioned in the baroque style. My grandfather had the only key to that chest and sometimes he would open it up and take out the only thing in it to show to us children. It was a parchment scroll that detailed the genealogy of our family going back four hundred years in Poland. That disappeared in the war.

Along with my own family and my grandfather, two of my father's siblings and their families also lived in the same building, my father's elder brother Zalman and my father's middle sister, Chana Lipsker. Zalman was regarded as a bit of a black sheep. It was a complicated story as to why; being a child, I didn't really know exactly what the details were. I think it had something to do with the fact that after his wife died, Zalman remarried and didn't look after his first wife's children, Noah and Shifra, very well. My father became like a guardian to them, and Shifra even got married in our house instead of her father's. I remember the wedding because of one awful incident: Women were hired to prepare the food for the wedding party in our apartment and one of the dishes they were preparing was called, in Polish, *galareta*, and in Yiddish, *p'tcha*; this was an aspic usually made from calves' feet, but ours was made from ox feet. It seems that, instead of using salt to clean the feet, they used, by mistake, way too much saltpetre, a chemical blend often used to preserve food. All the many people at the party ate this *galareta*, of course not knowing what the women had done, and suddenly, people started vomiting. A lot of people got sick but thankfully, nobody died.

My aunt Chana's husband was also a Hasid and he used to study a lot but I don't think he did much otherwise, in terms of work. He was a kind man but they always had money problems. Whenever they were badly off or had problems, Ciocia Chana would come to our house, lie on the sofa and say she had problems with her liver. "Ikh khalesh avek," she would moan in Yiddish, "I'm passing out," and she would ask for cocoa. When she did that, everybody knew that what she really needed was money. My father was always generous to her, so I don't think they were ever completely destitute.

My father's eldest sister, Esther, and her husband, Moishe Shlome Levinson, didn't live too far away. Moishe Shlome also came from a long line of Hasidim. He was originally from Warsaw but moved to

Lodz when he married my aunt and he then worked with my father and grandfather in the winemaking business. I don't recall what his actual role was but he was the only one in the family, other than my father and grandfather, who was involved in the business itself.

My youngest aunt, Sabina, was married to a man named Vovo Shpiegelglas and they lived in Warsaw. I don't know what he did for a living but they were wealthy and he used to come to visit us in Lodz, driving his own little Fiat motorcar, which had only two doors and red upholstery. My grandfather didn't like it when he came with his own car because, at that time, most people only had horses and *dro-shke,* a wagon, and my grandfather felt it was too showy for him to arrive in an automobile that he owned. "Farvus darfst du shtekn in di oygn?" my grandfather would say to him in Yiddish. Why do you want to rub it in? Why incur jealousy by sticking your wealth in their eyes?

My mother's family came from nearby a small town called Wieluń. Hers was also a Hasidic family and my maternal grandfather was a *cohen*, meaning that he was from a priestly tribe, and he was a very learned man. They too followed the Gerrer Rebbe, and that's how my parents ended up together. My father didn't know my mother before they got married. It was a *shidduch*, an arranged marriage, which had to be sanctioned by the Gerrer Rebbe. When they both went to meet with him the Gerrer Rebbe approved their marriage because both had *yiches,* good ancestry, and so it was considered a proper match. That's the way it was in those days. If you were a Hasid and close to the Rebbe, he had to look at the *yiches,* the pedigree, of the pro- spective bride or groom to determine if it was a suitable match. The important aspect of one's ancestry wasn't money, though — it was learning. The more sages you had in your ancestry, the more *yiches* you had and the more desirable you were for a marriage.

My maternal grandparents were both much younger than my pa- ternal grandparents and lived outside Wieluń, where they had a farm. I recall my grandmother Mirel putting fruit in jars, making jam and rendering fat for cooking. My grandfather, Shimshon Zilbersztajn, was tall and strong. The whole family was tall, with blond hair and blue eyes. In addition to the farm, my grandfather also had a tobacco shop in Wieluń. I only learned that fact when I went back to Poland many years after the war. The director of the archives in Wieluń informed me that it was impossible for my grandfather to have had a farm because Jews weren't allowed to have farms, but that he did have a tobacco shop in town. But the director was wrong — I had been to my grandparents' farm many times as a child, and my sister and I used to play with the chickens, geese, ducks and horses. My grandfather even exported eggs to England and I saw how they were packed in preservatives to keep them fresh for transport.

My mother, Chaja Jenta (Helena) Zilbersztajn Gutter, was born in 1908 and was the eldest of her siblings. She was beautiful, with her blond hair and blue eyes, which were passed down to both my sister and me, and was always extremely well groomed. She would have been considered quite a modern woman for her time because she didn't cut her hair as most religious women did and wore her *sheitel*, her wig, only in public, never at home. When she went out, she tucked her own hair under it. My mother was highly intelligent; she had a secular education and finished *Gymnasium*, the equivalent to high school, before the war. In fact, the Gerrer Rebbe encouraged secular education for women, which was rare at the time, and a lot of Hasidic women went to *Gymnasium*. In our Hasidic world, a lot of the women were secularly oriented while the men were religious and sheltered from worldly things, mainly devoted to work and study.

My mother spoke Polish fluently, and although we spoke Yiddish at home with my father, she spoke to my sister and I in Polish, so we were bilingual from birth. She was a voracious reader and often read books in Polish. I suppose I inherited my love of books from her. She encouraged me to read and bought me comics in Yiddish. She also bought me the comic book *Zorro* in Polish, and others as well. My mother took me to the cinema sometimes, a place where, if my father had known, I wouldn't have been allowed to go. Even my reading of comic books was without my father's knowledge, since he wouldn't have approved of me reading those books. All he wanted was for me to study the Talmud and the Torah, the Bible, and the commentaries of Rashi.

My father, Menachem Mendel Yonathan Gutter, was the second youngest in his family and was born in 1904 or 1905. He was a kind, charitable man. My grandfather would always say to him, "One day someone will take the shirt off your back." Every day, people would come and ask him for money and he would give his money away. But I think he was also a reticent, shy person. He was quiet and did not get involved in arguments. He was devoutly religious, and I always remember him with his head in a book. He hardly spoke Polish, mainly Yiddish and Hebrew, and was strict with me as far as study was concerned. The only time we really interacted was on Shabbos, the Sabbath, when I used to go with him down to the *shtiebl*, the house of prayer that was downstairs in our building. Most buildings had a *shtiebl*. People didn't go regularly to a shul, a synagogue. On the Sabbath, our neighbourhood looked like Jerusalem, with everybody walking with their *taleisim*, their prayer shawls. There were 250,000 Jews living in Lodz before the war, and our presence was felt.

Even though my father worked every day of the week and I saw little of him, his routine is strongly engraved in my brain. He would get up early in the morning and do his ablutions, his ritual wash, and then sit down and study the Talmud. After that, he would put on his *tallis*, his prayer shawl, and *daven,* pray. Only when he was done would he sit down and have his breakfast. As a small child, I would get up early too, and I would crawl underneath the table where he was sitting. He liked cigars, and as I sat there I would inhale the pungent aroma of his cigars. Every cigar had a ring on it and he would give me the ring to play with. When he finished a box of cigars, I would get the boxes, too. After his breakfast, my father went to the winery and was there all day. In the evening, he came back, studied some more and went to the *shtiebl*.

Our family's wine business was called *Złote Grono*, the Golden Grape, and on the logo was two people carrying a vine of grapes. We were the only Jewish winemakers in Lodz and one of the largest suppliers of spirits and wine in the country, as well as concessionaires of Stock brandies and liquors. Mainly we made kosher wine, but we also produced lots of wine from berries and other fruits, peach brandy and wine from honey. Our wine cellar was located at ulica Nowomiejska 19, about a ten-minute walk from our home. My grandfather and father imported the must, the freshly pressed grape juice, from vineyards in Hungary and brought it to the cellar in Lodz to make wine. I know that, at one time, my grandfather also owned vineyards in British Mandate Palestine; he used to go there once a year. Apparently, the last time he went to Palestine, which was in about 1938, he saw young Jewish women wearing short pants working in the vineyards. To my grandfather, as a Hasidic Jew, they didn't look modest, and he decided that it wasn't the right time for Jews to be in Palestine. We had to wait for the messiah to come first. So he sold the vineyards and bought some other properties but I don't know what type of properties or where they were.

We had a comfortable life when I was a small child. We had a large apartment on the first level above the ground floor that had a view of the street and of the garden in the central courtyard. When I looked out of my parents' bedroom window, I could see a textile factory across the road. We had five rooms, one of which was a large dining room with an enormous table that could comfortably seat between twelve and fifteen but could accommodate up to twenty-four people; our parents' bedroom; a shared bedroom for Sabina and me; a kitchen; and a toilet; and we also had a large balcony where we built the sukkah every year. My mother had a cook and servants to look after us children and we even had a telephone at home, which was unusual.

It was a wonderful life. Every Shabbos was like a special holiday and my mother would always make fish, soup, meat and compote. My father was a charitable person and would bring people to our house every Friday night for Shabbos dinner. On Saturday, there was always cholent for the midday meal. My mother would prepare this bean and meat casserole on Fridays and take it to the bakery, where it would cook overnight in the oven. Then, after prayers the next day, my sister and I would run to the bakery to collect it. We had a little piece of paper with a number written on it that we would give to the baker, and in return he would give us my mother's big pot of cholent. My sister would take one side and I would take the other and we would run home quickly because lunch needed to be served. As we ran, we anticipated the aroma and the delicious meat and barley, beans and potatoes; we also knew that nestled inside the cholent there was a little sealed ceramic pot with a sweet kugel for dessert.

To prepare for the beautiful Jewish holidays, the *Yamim Tovim*, my mother would be in the kitchen for weeks and we children were giddy with excitement, knowing all the family would be coming together to celebrate. In the summers, we went to our *dacha*, our summer house, which was in the forest at a place called Wiśniowa Góra, Cherry Mountain, about fourteen kilometres southeast of Lodz. My mother, my sister and I would stay there during the week and then my father would come out on Friday afternoons for the weekend. It was a place where a lot of other Hasidim went and I have memories of us all praying in the forest.

Because, as I mentioned, we were well off, Sabina and I had nannies. When we were young, my sister and I slept in the same room and had one nanny, who was Jewish. Sabina's cot was at one end of the room and mine was at the other, by the door, and in the mornings the nanny would bring little potties for us to use. As twins, we were like one person and always together. My sister had beautiful long blond hair to her waist that she was very proud of and wore in braids. My earliest memories are of us playing together. I was a naughty little boy and would pull her braids to tease her. I also remember that when she was ill, she didn't like to take medicine. I was better at it but she had to be coaxed to take it.

When I was three or three-and-a-half years old, my grandfather took me to cheder, religious school, for the first time. That first day at cheder, he took with him a bag of sweets. All the boys were sitting on low benches against a wall and I took the bag of sweets and gave each of the children a candy. Then my grandfather introduced me to the teacher. Being in a religious community, girls and boys were separated at an early age and the moment I started going to cheder, I became one of the men and my sister and I were separated. It became difficult for us to stay close; we each now had our own room and our own nanny. Sometimes my mother would take both of us to the park together, which was about a ten-minute walk from our house, but I rarely remember Sabina and I being taken out together by our nannies. The reason I specifically recall going to the park alone with my nanny is that she had a soldier boyfriend whom she would meet in the park when she took me out. In Poland, before the war, Jews had to do military service like everyone else and her soldier boyfriend was always wearing his uniform. I recall playing with the tiny metal ball that hung from the bottom of the bayonet attached to the back of his belt. While he was talking to my nanny, I would fiddle with this metal ball, intrigued by it.

At cheder I began to learn the *aleph-bet,* the Hebrew alphabet, as well as the Old Testament. There was a government regulation that we also had to learn secular subjects, so we learned Jewish subjects in the morning and secular subjects like reading Polish and simple arithmetic in the afternoon. My mother, as I mentioned, supplied me with comics in Polish to read at home so I learned Polish quickly, and by the age of five I was quite fluent in both Yiddish and Polish and understood a lot of Hebrew from my cheder studies. I went to school for only four years before the war started and that is all the formal education I had until decades later, after I got married. Everything else I know is self-taught and mostly learned from reading.

Once I started learning the Old Testament, and later on, when I began studying the Talmud, I was preoccupied with study; it was a big part of my life. Most important for me was to accurately learn the *parshah*, the weekly portion of the Bible, every week as well as Rashi's commentaries about it because when my father came home from work, he would often ask me what I had studied that day. He was so studious — he practically knew the whole Old Testament and Talmud by heart — and would test me on what I had learned at school. I didn't enjoy that because it felt like homework. If that wasn't bad enough, my grandfather sometimes asked me too. If I didn't know, the experience would be very unpleasant. I didn't like studying much and I especially didn't like being interrogated by my father and grandfather.

As a matter of fact, I did not like to follow rules. I didn't even like to say my prayers, either in the morning or in the evening. I knew I had to say my prayers just like my father did, before I could have breakfast, but I was stubborn and didn't want to. Eventually, I even developed a system to avoid saying them. I would hide in the washroom and my mother would come and knock on the door and say, "You must come out and say your prayers and if you don't, you will have to go to school without breakfast." But I was so obstinate that sometimes I wouldn't come out until it was time to go to school and then, true to her word, I had to go to school hungry.

At about the same time as I began going to cheder, my father took me down to the wine cellar and started to teach me how to become a winemaker. The first time, he took out ten bottles of wine, each one with a number painted on it from one to ten, and ten little cups the size of shot glasses. Then he poured a little wine into each of the cups and put it next to the bottle and said, "Go and inhale the aromas. Take your time and smell each one." I inhaled the aromas, but, as a little boy without patience, it didn't take long before I said I was done. Then he asked me to turn around so I couldn't see what he was doing. He took all the bottles away and mixed up the cups. Then he told me to turn back around, gave me one of the cups and told me to inhale the aroma. "Which bottle did that cup of wine came from?" he asked. Of course, I didn't know. But as time went by, I began to recognize what grape the wine was made from, which country it came from, what kind of mixture it was and so forth. That is the mark of a winemaker. The aroma is far more important than the taste. You have to really inhale the aroma of the wine to know what it is. I'm not a winemaker but even to this day, I can still tell, more or less, what grape a wine is from and also if it's good or bad just from the scent of the wine. My father taught me how to do that. By swirling the wine and inhaling it, whether the wine is red or white, I can tell if it's a fine wine, a young wine, or raw and not particularly great.

In my early years, the person I was closest to was my mother. I was a curious child, interested in seeing everything that was going on, and I was always around my mother, particularly when she was in the kitchen. I learned how to cook from her and I was actually in the kitchen with her more than my sister was. I can still visualize the kitchen and the window where she used to cool geese that she roasted. I can even recall how she used to control the heat on the wood-fired oven by putting rings on the burners depending on how hot she needed it to be. When she put all the rings on, there was low heat. If she wanted it hotter, she would take off the first ring and so on. I loved to watch her cook. Even though she had a cook, she did a lot of the cooking herself and supervised what the cook did. Her mother used to send her goose skins by train from the farm, which my mother would render into fat, *gribenes*. All our food was made at home and my mother always prepared the food for Shabbos and the Jewish holidays herself. I still make some dishes that I learned from watching my mother when I was five, six and seven years old. I make her cholent exactly the way she made it for my family.

At Passover, we couldn't eat anything made of matzah meal if it had touched any liquid. That meant we couldn't have regular noodles with our soup so my mother would take eggs, beat them and fry them thinly, like an omelette, and cut them into long strip-like noodles. Then she would throw these strips of fried egg into the chicken soup when she spooned it out. We also used to have something in the soup called *chremzlach*, a mixture of potato and egg fried in goose fat. She used to make cakes too, from almond flour or potato flour, and *bubas*, fried egg and potato flour balls that we put sugar on and had as dessert. On the eighth day of the holiday, we were finally allowed *kneidlach*, matzah balls, with our soup; although matzah meal or flour couldn't touch liquid on the first seven days of Passover, when the holiday was practically over, it was allowed. So on the eighth day my mother would go *meshugah*, crazy, with the matzah meal because she was allowed to use it to bake and to make *bubas*, *kneidlach* and *matzah brei*, matzah soaked in boiling water, drained and fried with egg. We children always looked forward to that last day of Passover — food made with matzah meal was so much tastier than that made with potato flour.

Every year, when my father observed his mother's *yahrzeit*, the anniversary of her death, my mother would make a huge meal for all of my father's Hasidic friends. Having such a large meal, in retrospect, was a funny tradition and may perhaps have been taken from Christianity, wherein ceremonies like wakes have such large gatherings. For that particular meal, she used to make what we called an *indik mitn krop*, a turkey with its crop, which is the swelling on the throat. I can envision both its appearance and taste. She used to carefully skin a turkey to keep it intact, take out all the meat, mince it and stuff it back into the skin. It still looked like a turkey, but it had no bones; my mother then baked it and cut it into slices like you would sausage.

Preparing for Shabbos started every Thursday. I would go with my mother to the market to buy fish, always live carp, which she would put in our bathtub so it could swim around for the night. Carp are bottom feeders and kind of muddy, so this gave the carp time to filter out all the impurities before she cooked it. On Friday mornings she would prepare the fish, chicken soup and noodles, which she would make herself, and either roast goose, chicken or veal. Then she would prepare the cholent for Saturday.

Whenever my mother got a goose from her mother for Shabbos, she roasted it and then put it beside the window to cool off before she put it in the ice chest, which contained a block of ice; we didn't have refrigerators in those days. I had a healthy appetite when I was a child and one day, there was this magnificent goose lying by the window and the smell was intoxicating. I couldn't resist it, and so, when nobody was looking, I tore a leg off and helped myself. After a while, my mother went to have a look at the goose. She glanced from the goose to me and said, "What happened to the leg?" I remember, as clearly as anything, answering, "The goose only had one leg." Of course, she knew exactly what had happened to that leg! I loved goose.

But there were certain things that I didn't like to eat, one of which was noodles. My mother, as she did for Passover, made her own, rolling the dough and cutting the noodles. When I refused to eat them, she would run after me with a spoonful of those noodles and when she caught up with me, she would force the noodles into my mouth, but I would keep them stuffed in my cheeks. In Polish, the word for swallow is *polknie* and when I was a child everyone used to call me Pinek. My mother was always running after me with these noodles saying, "Pinek, polknie," and after a while people were calling me Polknie Pinek. So, my nickname came from not swallowing noodles.

When I was six years old, I got quite ill with double pneumonia. In those days, pneumonia meant almost certain death and my parents must have been panic-stricken. I was put into my mother's bed right away. My mother constantly paced the bedroom, reciting psalms. Polish Jews were very superstitious, as were many Catholics, and my parents tried all kinds of superstitious remedies. They brought a white dove into the bedroom that flew around the room, did its business on the bed and made a nest on top of the wardrobe. I don't know exactly what the dove was supposed to be doing. As far as medicine was concerned, Dr. Hershvinkel, our family doctor, tried various remedies in the beginning but they didn't work. He applied hot *gehakte bankes*, cupping glasses, after making small cuts on my back; my back bled a bit and these heated cups were placed on top of the cuts to draw out the blood. They didn't help — the only result was that my back was terribly sore. The doctor also tried taking blood from my father and injecting it into my buttocks, which also had no effect.

Then Dr. Hershvinkel gave me some tablets. I had heard my parents talking about Dr. Hershvinkel going to Vienna to get special pills for me; once I began taking them, I coughed up buckets of phlegm and slowly began to recover. The tablets had MB imprinted on them and after the war I was told that they had been made by the May & Baker Company and that they were the first sulfa (*sulfonamide*) drugs. Those drugs saved my life.

Even after I was more or less recovered, my lungs remained pretty weak. I was sent to a place called Szczawnica, a spa resort town in Nowy Targ County in southern Poland famous for its clean air and waters rich in mineral salts. It is on the border between Czechoslovakia and Poland, located on the Dunajec River and near the Tatra Mountains. Szczawnica specialized in treatments of respiratory tract illnesses and people went there, as they do today, to be cured. Many Hasidim went there too, even the Gerrer Rebbe and his entourage.

The people living on the mountain above the village were Polish Christian mountain people called the Górale. They wore black hats with a feather and seashells sewn on the brims. They also had colourful clothes that they wore only on Sundays. The Górale lived in primitive huts alongside their animals. My mother brought me there and I think she stayed with me for a day or so, but then I was left alone with a family. My mother visited me and I think that my sister, Sabina, also came once. My father would come too, from time to time, but for the most part I was free to run around, left alone to be by myself surrounded by the mountains and the deep, cold river. That environment allowed me do things on my own that I'd never done before — being free, wandering and exploring — and I was very happy there. It felt as though time stood still, but I must have stayed there for about six months because I remember the changing of the seasons. Being so ill and then having a chance to recover must have been important to my psyche. Being alone, not in the bosom of my family and separated from my sister, left a great impression on me and shaped me in some way. I think this kind of self-reliance helped me survive later on.

There was one incident, though, that occurred during my time in Szczawnica that has stayed clear in my memory. There was a big park in the village down the mountain from where I was staying, and in the park there was a bandstand where, every Sunday, the bands of the local military or fire brigade used to come and play music. The music ranged from waltzes to opera, and because I always loved to listen to music, I would go there, sit on a bench and listen. Before each song, the bandleader would announce the name of the piece they were about to play. I have an especially poignant memory of a piece called *Śmierć Niewolnicy*, "Death of the Slaves."

By the time the concerts were over and I walked back up the mountain to the hut, it would be late in the day. Halfway between the park in the village and the mountains was a beautiful church and as I walked back, I would stop to listen to the music and the choir singing at the mass. I would stand outside and listen, captivated by the wonderful sounds. I knew I wouldn't be welcome inside with my blond *peyes*, sidelocks, and besides, as a Jewish boy, I wouldn't go inside a church anyway, so I stood at a bit of a distance and listened to the magnificent melodies.

On one particular Sunday, I was standing near the church and was so immersed in the music that I found myself walking closer to the church than I normally did to hear the music better. There were three or four steps leading up to the church door, and as I came to the first step, I must have been caught in a kind of rapture because I knelt on the first step to listen. Suddenly, I felt someone smack me hard on the back of the head. A middle-aged man had come up behind me and hit me. "How dare you contaminate the soil of our Holy Mother Church?" he said. The words he used were, *paskudny Żyd*, leprous, or filthy, Jew. Poland is a deeply religious, Catholic country and Mary, the mother of Jesus, is very important to there. So, to him, I suppose I was defiling the Holy Mother's church. I was so young that, at the time, I didn't think this incident really made that much of an impression on me. I simply ran back up the mountain to the family and their hut. Yet, I'm now sure the incident had some kind of an effect on me because it has stayed with me my entire life. I must have been frightened when the man hit me, as immersed in the music as I was. Yet I don't think it made me permanently afraid of everyone.

I wanted to make sure that I remembered this incident correctly, especially since I have recounted this story to people many times. The first time I went back to Poland, I didn't go back to my hometown of Lodz right away. I wanted to go back to Szczawnica to make sure that my memory of that time was precise. Was there really a church? Did it have steps? Was there a bandstand in the park? And when I went back, I saw that there was. It was just as I remembered. The bandstand was bricked up but it was there and so was the church. I was there in that village, I knelt on the church steps, I received a blow to the head and was chased away and I was called a dirty Jew. It wasn't my imagination.

People talk a lot about antisemitism in Poland before the war, but I didn't really see that much of it myself. I was a child, and fortunately for me I was growing up in a family that was reasonably well-to-do, so I was protected from lots of issues. Besides, I was busy with school and playing and making mischief and I didn't pay attention to much else. Still, even though I was preoccupied with my own thoughts and protected by my family, occasionally I was confronted by the difference between "us" and "them." Sometimes on my way home from cheder, young gentile boys would pull my *peyes* or they would shout, "Żyd idzie do Palestyny," Jew go to Palestine. Nonetheless, I always walked to cheder by myself. I never got the impression that my parents felt I was being threatened. There was certainly antisemitism between the two world wars and persecution of minorities (even though Jews counted between 10 and 12 per cent of the population, we were still considered a minority), but at the same time, we lived a decent life. In Poland, Jews worked in a myriad of occupations — as members of parliament and of the senate, doctors, lawyers, on the police force, as shop owners and for the radio station as well.

Yet, that said, life was not without its difficulties if you were a Jew. The concession for winemakers was awarded yearly and the input of ministers and others was needed to get the award. My father would phone the few Jewish members of parliament and rabbis with influence for weeks before the deadline every year. There was plenty of tension at home until he got all the people on board to intercede for him with the ministry and award him the concession for the coming year. There was a certain amount of bribery involved too, for those who didn't like Jews and others who could be influenced with a little help. Imagine people needing to do this every single year, knowing that their livelihoods could be cut off at the whim of ministers and officials, knowing that they were at the mercy of the caprice of these individuals.

There was one antisemitic incident that occurred to me and my mother but I think it may have had a greater effect on her than on me. One autumn day, we were out walking on our street. As always, she was beautifully dressed and was wearing her blond *sheitel* with her own beautiful blond hair tucked under it so you couldn't tell whether it was a wig or her own hair. I was walking next to her and holding her hand, wearing a little jacket and hat, my blond *peyes* sticking out of it. A man was coming toward us on the street and I still know exactly what he looked like: he was wearing a coat with a brown fur collar and he had on a brown felt hat; he wore a cravat at his neck; he had glasses on; and he walked with a cane that had a silver knob. As he approached, he stopped. My mother thought he wanted to ask her something but he just stared from her to me and then said to her in Polish, "How could a young beautiful woman like you work for these dirty Jews as a maid?" He had assumed that since my mother had blond hair and blue eyes she couldn't possibly be Jewish. My mother didn't say a word and we simply crossed the road. From that time on, if she saw anyone who seemed suspicious, we would cross the road to avoid them. We would even cross the road occasionally when we didn't need to and zigzag our way down the street. Certainly, life got worse as the war came closer. I had "Aryan" looks aside from my *peyes* and my mother started tying them up and putting them under my hat to hide them because, when we walked on the street, young gentile boys would come up to me and pull them. It reached the point that, by 1938, my parents wanted to immigrate to Palestine. I remember talk in the house about it but my grandfather objected to the idea and my parents wouldn't have disobeyed his wishes — their patriarchal deference was much too strong.

All these occurrences brought home to me the true relationship between Jews and gentiles in Poland, and although this thought stayed with me, I don't remember having emotions around it, in the same way that being chased from the church didn't disturb me to the extent that I thought that I had to be afraid in the world. It wasn't that I never felt anything — I do remember having lots of other emotions: how happy I was when my sister and I ran to get the cholent on Shabbos, the comforting smells of my mother's cooking.

Antisemitic incidents affected me only momentarily. I knew that Jews were not thought of highly by Catholics and that gentiles didn't like us. I knew we were separate but that was fine by me. My attitude was, so what? It didn't really bother me in my world. Until the war broke out, I had an idyllic childhood. I was surrounded by a loving family, I went to school, we weren't poor and I was being taught to be a respectable worker with a profession, a master winemaker, in a business that had been passed down in our family from father to son for generations.

Then the Nazis came in, and everything disappeared.

Darkness

Before the war, there was a lot of talk at home about Hitler. Caricatures of Hitler began appearing in the Yiddish papers, and some articles suggested that life would be hard for our men if they did not run away. Even my father decided to leave, and he starting walking to the Soviet Union. But he soon came back. I don't think he could bear to abandon his family. In my family, nobody ran away. I don't know whether they had the means to flee, and they had families to look after. But a lot of men left. Lots of people escaped, mostly to the Soviet Union, people with money who got smuggled out. At the time, no one knew that only weeks later the war would begin and the Soviets would take over part of Poland; they would ultimately send people who refused to take on Soviet citizenship to Siberia and other places in the harsh interiors of the Soviet Union. Some people survived Siberia; others died there.

The Gerrer Rebbe and his immediate family did manage to escape Poland. For the first several months after the Nazis occupied Poland, the Germans were looking for him because he was one of the most important sages and leaders of the Jewish Hasidic community and was respected not only by the whole Jewish community but also by the Polish community. After the war, I heard that, at the same time that one group of Gestapo officers was tasked with arresting him, a prominent group of his supporters succeeded in smuggling him and his family out of Poland. In 1959, a short book was published in Hebrew called *Nes hatzala shel HaRebbe MiGer,* The Miraculous Rescue of the Rebbe of Ger, and it tells how, in April 1940, he and his family boarded a train that left Warsaw for Italy; from there, a ship got them to Eretz Yisrael, the Land of Israel.

All that encompassed our life before the war came to an end on September 1, 1939, when I was just seven years old. On the first day of the war, my mother and I were on a train from Szczawnica to Lodz. My parents had sent me back to Szczawnica a second time, I don't know why exactly, but this time the Gerrer Rebbe was there with his entourage. I was on a boat with him on the Dunajec River; he and several of his followers were sitting in the back of the open boat on a wooden bench discussing the Torah. I, meanwhile, was flitting about, fascinated by the fast-moving river and the man who was rowing us on it. I even asked him if I could hold the oar and row. My grandfather was already sick by this time and my father had given me a supplication to give to the Rebbe, who said to me in Yiddish, "The Almighty will help him make a full recovery."

That first day, there was a lot of traffic. Suddenly, airplanes appeared and began strafing the train. The train stopped and everyone got off and ran to the ditches to hide. When the raid stopped, we got back on the train and it continued on, but the strafing occurred a few more times before we got to Lodz. My memory of getting off the train during the air raids is vague, but I recall the panic of the crowd. I don't remember being frightened when the train was being strafed by airplane fire. I was never frightened when I was a child. I reacted to tensions I felt from my parents, but I don't recall ever having the emotion of being terribly frightened myself.

We finally reached home and the next real memory I have is of what was going on in the house. I didn't quite understand it at the time but my parents, especially my mother, were extremely tense. I could feel the enormous sense of tension. My mother's family — her parents, her brother, his wife and child and her sister — all lived in

Wieluń, which was near the German border, and she hadn't heard from them. When they still hadn't arrived for Rosh Hashanah, which was almost two weeks after the war started, my mother was beside herself. There is an expression in Yiddish, *Choshech Mitzrayim*, literally, "darkness in Egypt," that comes from Hebrew and means pitch-black darkness, reflecting one of the plagues in Egypt. That's what my mother kept saying as she walked around the house.

Eventually, they did all arrive. We were so relieved. I recall seeing my grandparents, Shimshon and Mirel, my uncle, his wife and their baby, and my mother's younger sister who wasn't married at the time. Much later, I learned that Wieluń had been under siege on the very first day of the war and that much of the population, both Jewish and gentile, had fled as the army came in, which was probably why my extended family hadn't been able to communicate with my mother.

The first time that I really felt fear was about seven or eight days after the war started. I have no memory of real time then, but I know from research that the Nazis arrived in Lodz on September 8. Since they had no opposition, there had been no bombing in Lodz and the Germans came in quickly. Nazi officials compiled a list of prominent people in Lodz, Jews and non-Jews, and immediately went about rounding them up. My grandfather, as the head of a yeshiva, as well as of an organization called Machzikei Hadat, Upholders of the Faith, was on that list. I found documents after the war that proved he was involved in this organization, which worked to keep faith strong among Jews, and that is why he was on the Nazis' list.

At this time, my grandfather was seventy-eight years old and re-cuperating from a recent operation to remove kidney stones. He was lying in bed, still sick and weak, when the doorbell of his apartment rang. Since we lived next door to my grandfather, when his bell rang we heard it. My father, who was home because nobody was working due to the war, went over and opened the door; two men from the Gestapo, the Nazi Secret State Police, dressed in black mackintoshes, asked for my grandfather, Yitzhak Meir Gutter. My father led them into the bedroom, where my grandfather was. I was in the bedroom that day and I remember all of this quite clearly. When the men saw my grandfather, an old man with a grey beard, looking half-dead, they asked my father what was wrong with him and my father answered that he had recently had an operation and was very ill. I suppose they must have decided that it wasn't worth taking him since he didn't look like he was going to make it anyway, so they asked my father who he was and my father responded that he was the man's son. When they asked my father what he did for a living and heard he was a winemaker, they then asked him where he made the wine, and my father had to reveal the location.

The Gestapo took my father away. My mother, along with our whole family, was terrified, not knowing what was going to happen to him. My mother had always been a tense person, even before the war, which I had seen when I was ill, but from day one of the war, the light went out of her. We were told afterwards by our caretaker, who also looked after our wine cellar, that the Gestapo men had gone and ordered the gendarmerie, the military police, to stop at the cellar and help themselves to whatever was there. Apparently there were about 11,000 bottles of wine, whiskey and liquor, as well as the many vats where the wine was maturing. They took all the bottles and then broke open the vats and poured the wine out into empty jerry cans. When they finally left, the caretaker went down to the cellar and found my father badly beaten and lying unconscious in a corner. Curfew was in effect already and the caretaker risked his own life by carrying him home on his back. My father was unconscious for four or five days after that, but Dr. Hershvinkel, who had treated me when I was sick, helped him recover. That was my first encounter with the Nazis who, just forty-eight hours after they had arrived, had destroyed an enterprise generations of my family had built over almost one hundred years.

~

As the war was raging, the Zilbersztajns couldn't go back to Wieluń, so the whole family stayed with us in Lodz. But we weren't there much longer. After the experience he'd had in the wine cellar, my father was worried that the Nazis were going to come back. Besides, there was an enormous amount of terror against Jews in Lodz right from the beginning of the occupation. Every day there was a new law telling us what we were no longer allowed to do. Anyone who had a shop had to hand it over to an "Aryan." There were approximately one hundred thousand Germans living in Lodz, leftover from the Prussian and the Austro-Hungarian Empires; these people, who were Polish citizens, were called *Volksdeutsche,* ethnic Germans. They were given round swastika lapel pins to wear on their coats and distinguish them from everyone else, and they were allowed to take over shops owned by Jews. Any Jew who worked for the municipality or police, or who was a lawyer or other professional working for a firm, was fired. The Nazis froze the bank accounts of Jews. They began taking Jews to do forced labour and randomly rounded people up and killed them.

In November, we were informed that Lodz was going to be evacuated of all non-Germans, and my father decided to send us to Warsaw to stay with his sister, my aunt Sabina. Jews weren't allowed on the trains but we were blond, blue-eyed twins and my mother looked like a Scandinavian beauty. All three of us also spoke fluent Polish, so there was a good chance we wouldn't be detected. My parents told me they had to cut off my *peyes* for the trip but I began crying hysterically and refused to let them. My *peyes* were part of me and I couldn't imagine myself without them. My mother, persistent, chased me around the apartment and finally caught me and put me down on a chair. I cried as she took off my hat, chopped off my blond *peyes* with scissors and combed back my hair so I would look Polish. Then we packed some suitcases and went to the train station, where my mother instructed us to speak only Polish. It seemed as though everyone wanted to get out of Lodz — there were thousands of people trying to get on the trains. It took a long time to get tickets but we finally did, and then the train was so crowded that we had to stand because there were no seats.

There was a well-dressed, middle-aged German man on the train who took a shine to my mother. He began helping my mother with our parcels and got us seats in a compartment on the crowded train. I could see that my mother was terrified. He wouldn't leave us alone and kept talking to her all the way to Warsaw, no matter how she tried to put him off. When we finally arrived in Warsaw, he told her he had a limousine waiting for him and wanted to give us a ride to wherever we were going. My mother kept telling him that it wasn't necessary, that there would be someone waiting for us, but he didn't want to hear it and wouldn't take no for an answer. He said that his chauffeur would take us, and he grabbed our suitcases and put us in the limousine with him. When he asked where we were going and she replied ulica Elektoralna 14, an address that was in a predominantly Jewish area of Warsaw, his interest evaporated and he couldn't wait to get rid of us. He didn't kick us out exactly, but as soon as we neared the street, he threw us out with our suitcases.

Some other members of the family also came to Warsaw around the time we did, like my Uncle Zalman's son Noah and my father's eldest sister, Esther, and her husband, Moishe Shlome Levinson. Later on, we all spread out, but in the beginning, there were about seventeen people staying at the apartment of my aunt Sabina and uncle Vovo Shpiegelglas, including Sabina and her husband and their two children. Like my parents, they had a boy and a girl, but they were much older than my sister and I. When we got there, I was assigned to sleep in Aunt Sabina's daughter's room, where one whole wall was covered in bookcases. The books were mostly in Polish and some of them were textbooks because she had recently finished *Gymnasium*. I read them from cover to cover, even though I didn't always understand what I was reading. When more people began to arrive, there was less room and fewer beds for everyone so I slept on a cot in a corridor with Noah. It was a very cold winter that year, one of the coldest on record in Warsaw, and all the window glass had been blown out in the bombing so it was freezing. I mostly lay in bed under the covers and read in the crowded little apartment.

In either December 1939 or January 1940, the Germans did something that I didn't know was possible until it happened to us. One day, we were all lying in bed due to the cold. The windows were covered with cardboard or newspapers and we covered ourselves with shawls or blankets and duvets, whatever we could find. No one got up early, since we had nowhere to go. We simply stayed in bed trying to keep warm. It must have been nine or ten in the morning when suddenly the doorbell rang and three men dressed in black mackintoshes and hats, like the Gestapo wore, came barging into the apartment. They could have been anybody, really, Nazi security forces or regular police or even ordinary Germans. But, in the end, it didn't really matter. One of them took out a revolver and ordered us all to undress completely. He demanded that we stand facing the wall with our hands up against it and he said that if anyone turned around while they were there, he would shoot them dead on the spot.

We all did as we were told and stood there shivering. As a Hasidic boy, I had never seen anyone naked, especially not a woman. I had only ever seen a man without clothes when my father took me to the mikvah, the ritual bath, and then only by accident. Modesty was so important in our lives that, even if I had been able to look, I would have averted my eyes. And here was my eldest aunt, Ciocia Esther, who was fifty then and had grown-up children, and my aunt Sabina, who was much younger, my aunt and uncle Levinson and my cousins, even my mother and my sister, all of them naked. This scared me — not because I was worried that the men would hit me or kill me, but because I didn't understand what was going on. Life had been turned upside down.

We stood there for what seemed an eternity to me but must have been about twenty minutes to an hour while they ransacked the apartment. When they were finished, the same voice that had spoken before, the one with the revolver, said they were going to leave and we had better not move until they had banged the door shut and were gone. Otherwise, he said, he was going to shoot us all. As soon as they left, everyone dressed quickly and took in what they had done to the apartment. It was a mess and anything of value had been taken: the Shabbos candlesticks, the Kiddush cups, whatever they thought might have worth. I particularly remember the candlesticks because on Friday night, there was nothing to place the candles in for Shabbos.

The incident upset us all, but it didn't impact me to the extent that it did the grown-ups; I probably didn't fully grasp the meaning of what had happened. I continued with my reading, living mostly in my own head. When I wasn't reading, I was out in the streets. My sister never ventured outside — she barely left my mother's side — but I was always out in the streets. I was a blond, blue-eyed boy who spoke Polish perfectly, so I suppose that my mother wasn't that worried about letting me out and, luckily, nobody touched me. As for me, I wasn't afraid even though terrible events were swirling around me. I was taking it all in, so I don't know why I wasn't afraid. I think my mind just went blank. I had no feelings at all. I had disengaged myself from what was happening. It was as if my eyes were cameras and my brain was the screen. I just recorded everything, without emotion or participation.

What the Nazis had done in Lodz was now happening in Warsaw. The Nazis set up a Judenrat, a Jewish Community Council that was responsible for, among other things, gathering Jews for slave labour details. Sometimes the Judenrat had to deliver five or six thousand Jews every day; other times, it was hundreds. Warsaw had been badly damaged in the month-long bombardment at the beginning of the war and many buildings had been destroyed. Instead of using bulldozers, the Nazis used Jews to clear the rubble and repair the roads, the airports, which were now used by the military, and whatever else needed repair. Along with tradespeople and storekeepers, they took yeshiva *bochers,* young religious men, as well as doctors, lawyers and professionals — people who had never done any physical labour in their lives — and made them work as slaves in the streets. The Nazis immediately enlisted informers, of whom there were plenty, to find out who the rich and influential Jews were in the city.

Jews were subjected to all kinds of dreadful treatment and our situation quickly became chaotic. Jews had become outlaws. We weren't safe in the streets anymore. Even secular Jews, who may not have been recognizable as such, could be targeted by a Polish gentile, who might start pointing and saying, "Jude, Jude, Jude." (Jew, Jew, Jew.) Then, a German or Polish hooligan would often rob and beat the Jewish person. Anybody who wasn't Jewish could stop a Jew in the street and take what they wanted. I don't think most honest and decent people did that, but those who did were particularly danger- ous. When young hooligans saw a Jew, they would stop him and beat him, and if he had a watch, they would tear it off him or go through his pockets and take all his money. I saw them doing it.

From the start, there were so many rules and regulations restrict- ing Jews. We had to take off our hats when we saw a soldier; we couldn't go into the parks or walk on the pavement — we were forced to walk in the middle of the road; and we couldn't ride in regular streetcars. In the beginning, before the ghetto was established, there were specially designated streetcars for Jews, with a Jewish star on the front. There was rationing right away, too, so from the start it was difficult for Jews to buy food. When Jews came to a shop, they would get shoved to the end of the line or kicked out altogether, not only by the Germans, but also by the Poles.

My mother decided that in order for us to get food, I, as a Pol- ish-looking boy, would have to go to the shops. This made me, for the first six or eight weeks until my father came back, the provisions provider for the seventeen people who lived in my aunt's apartment. Some of the scenes I saw in Warsaw were horrific. Ordinary German soldiers on leave, not Nazis, amused themselves by collecting a few

Jews and cutting off their beards and even some skin underneath, making them bleed. Or they would grab young Jewish girls in the street and make them dance like monkeys. And the Polish police, or the "Blue Police," as we called them because they wore blue uniforms, would just stand by. I don't know whether they collaborated with the Nazis at first, but soon enough, as early as 1940, the Polish police collaborated happily. They didn't wait for the evacuations to begin or for the resettlements. Right from the beginning, you could do anything you wanted to a Jew. And they did.

The Observer

When my father finally arrived, at the beginning of 1940, everyone was still living at the apartment in Warsaw. He had walked from Lodz, a distance of about a hundred kilometres. My father had cut his hair and *peyes* but he spoke very little Polish and still had a closely cropped beard, so I don't know how he managed to travel without getting caught, especially since, at that time, a border had been established around Lodz, making it part of the greater German Reich, and he had had to smuggle himself out. The Nazis had big plans for Lodz and incorporated the city into the Reich so it would become part of Germany in a new area called Warthegau, or Wartheland. They changed the name of Lodz to Litzmannstadt and renamed all the streets in German. Their plan had been to expel all the Polish Jews and Polish gentiles from Lodz but it didn't work out because as they initiated the evacuation, there was such panic and chaos — transportation was a challenge and gathering places were mobbed — that they eventually decided to leave all the Polish gentiles in Lodz and establish a ghetto for the Jews.

I don't exactly know how my father managed to get through or what route he took to get to Warsaw but it took him about two months, a journey that today takes about forty-five minutes by car; in those days, it was three hours by train. He said that he walked at night and managed to hide during the day with friendly farmers. Poland was full of forests, so when he was in a forested area there was some protection; he was able to cover himself with leaves and snow so he could sleep during the day and have the strength to start walking again at night in the deep snow and freezing temperatures. Perhaps he sometimes managed to pay someone with a horse and buggy to give him a ride.

I'm sure the meeting with my father and his appearance at the apartment must have been emotional but, strangely, I don't remember it. I was a peculiar young boy, a bit of an introvert. I spent a lot of my time by myself, didn't have friends and didn't get involved in much. I observed quite a lot, and I feel that the most important things I saw or experienced are stuck in my memory. That's how I am to this day.

My father must have brought with him some money and jewellery to sell, because he was able to start searching for a place for us to live right away. Seventeen people couldn't continue to live together in that small apartment. He soon found a tiny apartment in a four- or five-storey building at the corner of ulice Nalewki and Mila. Ulica Mila later became a famous street during the Warsaw Ghetto Uprising, which started on April 19, 1943. Mila 18 was the headquarters of the underground uprising. The front of the building where our apartment was had been destroyed by a bomb at the beginning of the war but the three quadrants at the back were left intact and we lived on the side right next to the destroyed front. We used half of the apartment as a bedroom for the four of us and the other half as a kitchen. There was a toilet in the corner but the communal bathroom, which had a bathtub in it, was in the hallway.

Later on, once the ghetto was created in October 1940 and more people were forced into that area, the Judenrat allocated additional people to live in apartments that had two or three rooms; seven or eight people were put in a room, depending on its size. People didn't want to live like that and there was a lot of screaming and yelling but a lot of people couldn't even find places to live. We were lucky that our place was so small that the Judenrat couldn't push any more people in. But even though we didn't have anybody living with us on a day-to-day basis during the time of the ghetto, my father used to bring people to sleep on the floor at night if they had nowhere to go.

Once we moved into the apartment, my father had to find a way to make a living. He was a winemaker, that's what he knew how to do, and so he set up a winemaking operation in the kitchen of our tiny apartment. Before the ghetto was established, there was still a kind of quasi-normalcy in Warsaw and you could buy items on the black market if you had money, so he bought raisins and got a small barrel to ferment the raisins in with sugar. He managed to clarify the must and have the wine drip into another container through a contraption he made of four linen pouches. Then he'd add brown sugar to give the wine a colour that made it look like real Kiddush wine.

There was still a community of 350,000 Jews in Warsaw then who were making Friday night suppers, and they would order wine from him. I would put on my rucksack and deliver the wine in small or large bottles, depending on what they asked for, and collect the money. I don't know where my father got the corks — perhaps he bought them on the black market, too — but he enlisted me to go looking for empty bottles. I used to stand outside cafés and places where people threw out empty bottles and I would bring the bottles home. My father would immerse them in water for three days to make them kosher, and then he would take off the original labels.

He also found a little kiosk for my mother on the ground floor of a building not far from our apartment, also on ulica Nalewki, where she sold sweets and chocolates and cigarettes that people would buy individually or, if they had money, by the packet. You entered the kiosk by a narrow door at the back and stood and sold goods at the window, which faced the street. Since I was always running around the streets looking at what was going on, I would come into the kiosk by the little entrance at the back where there were a few shelves on which she stored the packets of candies and cigarettes. I always searched for one particular little sweet called Krówki, which means little cow, that was wrapped in yellow paper with a portrait of a cow; it was fudge made from condensed milk and sugar. I would steal these little sweets while my mother worked the window, and even though she always told me that I mustn't do that, she never stopped me and she looked away when she saw me taking them. In 2002, when I came back to Poland for the first time, I went into a sweets shop and there, in large glass containers, were these same little Krówki, exactly like the ones my mother had sold. I immediately felt as if my mother were standing right there in front of the window. That's how strongly I connected those candies to my mother.

So, my parents were making a living in our little apartment in Warsaw, where the four of us slept together in one bedroom. My mother sold sweets and cigarettes during the day and at night my father would make wine in the kitchen. In the meantime, Jews were being rounded up and beaten; our existence was constantly worsening. The rationing continued and it became difficult to get food like honey, jam and cooking oil. Everything was *ersatz,* made from ingredients other than the proper ones. My mother used to get artificial honey and jam that was made of beetroot. For cooking she could now only get rapeseed oil, which was not well refined and had a sickening smell and taste. Despite all that, because of my father's ability to provide for us, we never went hungry in Warsaw. Not in the ghetto, not ever. My parents, particularly my father, watched us like hawks. When I think of him now, it is as if he had angel's wings with which he gathered us in and guarded us as best he could. He was mild-mannered but quite brave. And when it came to his family, his main concern was to look after us and save us.

This life lasted for a little while and then, in the middle of 1940, people began talking about a ghetto. Fortunately, our apartment and my mother's little kiosk would be in the ghetto because Nalewki was one of the streets in Warsaw where many Jews lived, so we continued to live there right through until the end, even when the Warsaw ghetto was divided in half. In November 1940, the ghetto was closed and life grew much more difficult. My father somehow still managed to get raisins on the black market to make wine after the ghetto was closed off, but my mother's kiosk lasted for only another six months or so. Either she couldn't get the items she needed anymore or people didn't have any more money to buy them. It might also have been that it was too difficult for her to deal with the black market. Maybe she wasn't strong enough to hustle. Before the war, she was a lady who didn't work, so perhaps she could only work the kiosk as long as she didn't need to be too pushy, which she didn't have the mentality for.

After the kiosk closed, my mother would bake challah buns, which became the main source of income for our little family. On Thursdays or Fridays my parents would give me addresses and I would go round to deliver both wine and challahs and then bring back the money to them.

At that time, life in the Warsaw ghetto had the air of a schizophrenic normality. Although life was difficult, it wasn't so horrible that we couldn't live. For instance, schools were forbidden but they existed nonetheless. My father found a *melamed,* a teacher, who taught a few children in secret and I studied the Talmud with him. We studied the book *Nedarim,* or Vows, which is challenging with its *perush*, commentary, by Ran, the acronym for the name of Rabbi Nissim ben Reuven of Gerona. I looked forward to the diversion of those classes, and I liked the teacher. It was not systematic study, mainly discussion, and I enjoyed that as well. But it didn't last long.

Before the ghetto was closed, it was easier to get things on the black market because food wasn't that expensive and people could sell clothes or other belongings to the Poles. And people were still working, so the situation was not dire. But the moment the ghetto was closed, everything became difficult and restricted, especially the rationing of food, and hunger started to kill people. German civilians got 2,613 calories of official food rations a day but, truly, the Germans could go and help themselves to more if they wanted to; nobody was going to stop them. If a *Volksdeutsche* or German walked into a shop, no Polish shopkeeper was going to tell them that they couldn't have a loaf of bread or a piece of sausage. For Polish people, the rations were 699 calories a day, but for the Jews, the rations were 184, fewer calories than in a typical chocolate bar.

By the beginning of 1941, the situation deteriorated even more quickly and we started seeing dead bodies in the streets. At first only a few, but when more people were brought into the ghetto — at one point, 400,000 or more Jews were living in the ghetto, before the onset of "resettlement" — hundreds of people lay dying in the streets. Some people, desperate, would strip the bodies and sell their clothes to the Poles, who still had permission to come into the ghetto at that time, or exchange the items for food. The lack of sanitation was horrible and there was a tremendous amount of disease like tuberculosis, typhus and pneumonia. My uncle Moishe Shlome Levinson died during this time, I think from tuberculosis. My father attended his funeral and he was buried in the Warsaw ghetto cemetery.

There was a *chevra kadisha*, a burial society, in the ghetto, but with so many dead bodies in the streets, it became harder and harder for the society's members to bury them in individual graves; they had to dig a huge pit in the cemetery to accommodate the number of bodies they were faced with. The burial society didn't have enough people to help or enough wooden carts to wheel all the bodies to the cemetery, so they grabbed men off the streets to help and gave them wheelbarrows to pile the dead bodies in. One day, I saw a scene that no one should see. I watched as rows of people walked with wheelbarrows full of dead bodies to the cemetery and I saw them tip the bodies, some half-dressed and some naked, into the pit, like garbage. These poor souls had no Kaddish, the prayer for the dead, said for them or anything else required for a respectful Jewish burial. They were just bodies being dumped into a pit, like animals might be. In total, approximately 90,000 Jews died in the Warsaw ghetto of hunger and disease; the current Jewish cemetery in Warsaw still displays the pit, which is a mass grave and has become a depression in the earth because, when a body is buried, at first it moves as it bloats and then it disintegrates and becomes a skeleton, making the ground shift and collapse.

The Warsaw ghetto was mayhem: apocalyptic hell. The Judenrat organized what the Germans demanded and established a Jewish police force that wore blue bands around their police hats, a Jewish prison, a Jewish fire brigade and a Jewish post office. This gave us the semblance of self-government, but we weren't self-governed. The Gestapo would come every day and tell Adam Czerniaków, the head of the Judenrat, what we could and could not do and how many people to supply them for forced labour. There was also, for a short time, a group known as the "Jewish Gestapo" that comprised informers and collaborators who worked with the Germans. We called them the *trzynastka*, which is Polish for thirteen, because they had their own headquarters at ulica Leszno 13. They wore police hats with green bands on them to distinguish them from the many other groups put in place to keep the Jews in check.

The Nazis set up factories inside the ghetto in addition to those they already had outside the ghetto to produce for the war effort. On the inside, factories were set up to make uniforms, brushes, shoes and other things for the army. Jewish tailors, seamstresses and shoemakers were thus able to work and get a little bit of money and a little more food. But it still was not enough to feed a family.

I don't know what was being made outside the ghetto, but every day columns of Jews went out of the ghetto to work. I often stood at the ghetto gate where there were always two German gendarmes and Polish policemen standing on what was known as the "Aryan" side and Jewish policemen who stood on the inside of the gate, all watching to check that no one was trying to escape the work details. Sometimes Jews would be taken away for a week to work, and not all would come back.

There was death and despair at every turn. Profiteers and black marketeers took advantage of the situation and made money. It's ironic, but the collaborators and the smugglers saved a lot of people from hunger because they, together with the Nazis, brought food into the ghetto. There was nothing you couldn't get in the ghetto if you had money, including a proper burial in the cemetery. It was all about bribery and corruption and some people made money off the backs of those who were suffering. There were cafés where people played music and danced and drank wine. I would stand outside these cafés as I was rummaging for empty bottles and smell the geese being roasted, while two feet away there was a dead body lying in the street.

As a Hasidic boy, I didn't know of females and males and sex, but when I was standing outside one of these cafés where people were having fun, I would often see extremely well-dressed women walking up and down the street. Men would come up to them, they would talk for a few moments and then they would disappear together. Some twenty minutes or half an hour later, the women would come back and walk up and down the street again. I always wondered what kind of business they were doing. It took me years to understand what it was about.

So many terrible things were going on in the Warsaw ghetto in 1941 and the first half of 1942 that, if you weren't there, you really can't understand it. Even if you were there, you can't understand it. But I always say that it is important for people to know that, despite many in the Judenrat who did the bidding of the Nazis, the brutal Jewish police, the dreaded "Jewish Gestapo" and the profiteers, among them there were some who were not bad and did try to help. And there was always resistance to what was forbidden. There were lots of underground newspapers, underground schools for the children, universities where professors had smuggled in research materials and people were being taught, some of them to become doctors. People were able to send parcels from abroad and within Poland to the Jewish post office. I think that many of the parcels were stolen by the Germans, the Jewish police and the Jewish post office workers, but some of them did get through to the people who needed them. And there was an enormous amount of passive resistance in the Warsaw ghetto by people who risked their own existence to help others.

There was one man, a famous man by the name of Emanuel Ringelblum, who organized people to collect any information relating to ghetto life. His organization, Oneg Shabbat, buried thousands of archival documents in tin and milk cans, many of which, miraculously, were discovered after the war. By 1941, the food situation had become so dire that people were dying in the streets on a daily basis, and Ringelblum and his followers set up a soup kitchen to give people at least a bowl of soup and a piece of bread. His was not the only soup kitchen in the ghetto but setting these up was not easy to do. Wealthy Jews — and there were still quite a few then in the Warsaw ghetto — were urged or coerced into giving money to assist in buying bread and making the soup so that the starving could be fed. Synagogues and halls were opened to the homeless and every effort was made to try and help those who were living on the streets in the middle of winter.

As I mentioned, my father, too, did what he could by bringing people to our tiny apartment at night to sleep on the floor in the kitchen. I particularly remember one man who my father used to allow to sleep in our apartment. This man was covered in boils, and my mother would get angry and say to my father, "How can you bring him here? The kids are going to get ill!" But my father was such a good person, and he continued to do what he felt was right.

~

Even if this world exists for a thousand, million, trillion light-years, no one could ever be able to tell all the stories of the Warsaw ghetto during the years from 1940 until the end of the uprising in the middle of 1943. And I, this little boy, saw it all. I watched the depravity and the kindness, people doing business, children selling cigarettes, women prostituting themselves. I saw every aspect of humanity, from evil to goodness. I saw people living and dying in the streets, and Jewish police beating children who were trying to stay alive by stealing a potato and selling it. I saw Germans beating Jews and German officers conducting tours of the ghetto with cameras, smiling and laughing and pulling Jewish beards and *peyes* and giving out sweets to the children as if to little animals in a zoo. I was taking it in, but I couldn't truly comprehend. This made only a visual impact on me — not an emotional response but a physical reaction. As a child, I didn't have the intellect or the understanding to rationalize what I saw and I couldn't relate it to my experience of life up to that point. I simply photographed everything my eyes saw with an impersonal camera and stored these images in my brain. In a normal life, dying is a normal activity of the human race. You are born, you grow and become educated, hopefully you get married, have children and maybe grandchildren and then, if you are lucky, you live to a ripe old age and die. That's normal. But to me, back then, death was something you had to fight against. It was the enemy.

I had one friend during the time in the ghetto, a boy who lived in the apartment next to ours and who was the nephew of the Gerrer Rebbe. We spent time together, playing in the yard and talking. He died sometime in 1942, and I saw people perform the ritual washing of his body in the bathroom everyone on our floor used for bathing. Seeing the water flow down the drain felt to me like his life, his soul, was literally going down the drain as well. I still, to this day, cannot have a bath because of this experience. This image made an enormous impression on me; it was particularly painful to me because I actually had a relationship with that boy. To me, there was a real person inside the body.

I was constantly surrounded by death; it felt like it cornered me, and this has damaged me to this day. I can't relate to death like other people do. Death was always, constantly, an enemy to fight. I have an extreme phobia toward death — it creates a kind of havoc inside me.

I was not concerned about being separated from the rest of the population. We had always been separate and lived separate lives. It was the extreme level of anxiety and the feelings that grown-ups always gave me that I had to be scared for my life. Whenever I saw a German I would run away. I knew that I had to be afraid. If I spied a German officer, a soldier or even an ordinary German walking or driving by, I would make myself scarce. A Jew had to take off his hat if he saw a German, and I didn't want to take off my hat. But if I tell you that it was because I was trying to send them a defiant message by not taking off my hat, it would be untrue. I knew that if I took off my hat they would notice me, and I didn't want to draw attention to myself. I believe this was the beginning of my discovering ways to make myself invisible. When I was later incarcerated in the concentration camps, I always tried to make myself invisible and stay away from anyone who might want to do me harm. It was self-defence. For the first time in my life I felt threatened as a human being and I was afraid. It was the feral fear of the unknown and of being powerless and alone in the face of mortal danger.

Life in the ghetto was, as I mentioned, schizophrenic. I don't know what else to call it. As time passed, more people were dying on the streets, and there were informers everywhere, ready to turn you in for any real or imagined infraction if it would get them an extra bite of bread. How anyone could possibly have survived in the Warsaw ghetto is still an absolute mystery to me. In order to survive at that time, my emotions and feelings shut down and to some extent have remained that way to this day. I cannot allow myself to let go, to be spontaneous. I always feel a sense of uncertainty and fear. I knew I could be killed in the ghetto and I knew that even more later, in the concentration camps and the death camps where I had to pray that no one notice me if I wanted to live through a day. This affected me. Although being able to shut myself off saved me, it also hurt me.

The Nightmare

Life continued to deteriorate in the ghetto throughout 1941 and the beginning of 1942. Then my father stopped making wine and my mother stopped baking challah buns. I don't know how they made a living after that but the change in our situation took an enormous toll on both my parents. My father's appearance didn't change that much — he still had his little scraggly beard — but he was weakening inside. Amazingly, though, he never lost his faith. And not only did he not lose his faith, but he remained deeply religious, even at the most desperate of times.

My mother, however, changed dramatically. I think it was very hard for her to accept that she had gone from being the educated lady of the house to where she was now. When we were in the ghetto, I don't remember ever seeing her smile. In my mind, I always see her as she was before the war when we walked in the streets of Lodz, when she had beautiful hair that she incorporated into her *sheitel*, when she wore fashionable hats and was always elegantly dressed. She was only in her early thirties when we were in the ghetto but her beautiful blond hair went a kind of dirty grey and she cut it short. She wanted to cut off my sister's hair, too, because of the lack of sanitary conditions, but my sister wouldn't let her. My mother became preoccupied and tense. Her parents and all her siblings were in the Lodz ghetto and she never heard from them and didn't know whether they were alive or dead, so one can imagine the trauma she was living with. She spent a lot of time in the toilet but I don't think she always went there because she needed to. I think she simply needed a few minutes to herself. The place was small and noisy and she wanted to be alone. She was worn down and showing great pain. I feel that she may have been unwell and suffering from some illness in the ghetto, particularly toward the end of 1941.

I think that my mother suffered the most from not knowing how to save her children. She was desperately trying to keep our family together and look after us. I was ill several times — not seriously ill — but I had weak lungs and got sick and had a fever for a long time. My parents made sacrifices and bought medication for me. They even tried to force me to eat horsemeat soup on the advice of a doctor and they somehow pushed it down my throat, even though I screamed and refused to eat it because it wasn't kosher. Even though I didn't like studying or praying except on my own terms, I was strongly committed to my faith.

On July 22, 1942, placards appeared on walls in the ghetto announcing the deportation of the Jews. I was ten years old by then and that was when I started to feel a real sense of hopelessness. It was as if there was an abyss in front of me. I wanted to be pulled back from it, and to this day I feel that there is a hand pulling me back into that abyss whenever I get depressed. Even though I live in a civilized world now, and hopefully I'll die in a civilized manner, there is still that chaotic cosmos in the back of my subconscious that comes out in all kinds of shapes in my nightmares. The feeling of there being a pit in front of me has never left me and I have to be on my guard against the unknown. I rarely allow myself the luxury of complete happiness, even at the happiest moments of my life. I have a tortured soul and that is my legacy from the Holocaust.

Soon after the placards appeared there was an announcement that in order to stay in the ghetto you needed to have documents stating you could work. I think my father got his documents first through

Rav (Rabbi) Avram Krol, who was a cousin of ours by marriage. He was an astute, brilliant man who knew how to organize matters and take care of himself. Rav Krol had a high position in one of the clothing factories in the ghetto and was on good terms with one of the German managers. Rav Krol often helped my parents by getting food, and I think that he even helped my father get raisins when he was still making wine. When he came to visit us, he would always bring items with him or he would be arranging something for us, and my father would hand over some jewellery in return.

Krol was a brave man who fought in the Warsaw Ghetto Uprising and was also in Warsaw during the city uprising in 1944. During the city uprising, he fell four storeys from a building and broke his arms and his legs. How he survived, God only knows. When the Soviets arrived in Warsaw, they took him to a hospital, where his bones were reset, but one of his legs withered and he walked with a limp.

The last time I saw Rav Krol in the ghetto was after the second deportation, when he came to our apartment to talk to my father. He told my father that it didn't matter what documents he brought us, the Germans had no intentions of leaving anyone alive in the Warsaw ghetto. He was sending his wife and children to the "Aryan" side because they were blond and blue-eyed, and he wanted my mother and my sister to go to the "Aryan" side too. But my mother refused and said she wasn't going anywhere without her husband and son. That I remember very clearly.

Even though the placards suggested that those living on the streets and those who were sick and didn't have food were going to be sent to a better place where they would be taken care of and fed, my father didn't believe it; he did not trust the Nazis at all. He understood that they were not going to send us to be taken care of; he understood that the Germans played games. They issued a number of different identification cards to those people who were to remain in the ghetto. Then they would have inspections to check those cards, and suddenly they would invalidate the original cards and issue new ones. They played this game time and time again as they continued to deport people on a regular basis.

Soon enough, people learned that the ones deported were being sent to Treblinka to be gassed to death in the showers. Within six weeks of the first deportations, everyone was talking about it. Those who were taken to the *Umschlagplatz*, the deportation square, were going to Treblinka to be murdered. Very few people were able to escape Treblinka — I knew of one who did by smuggling himself out by hiding in a wagon full of the clothing of murdered Jews. He came back and told us about the gas that came out of the spouts instead of water in the showers and the bodies that were being burned in open ditches. The smoke of the dead bodies permeated the whole area and even the farmers living in that area knew that the Nazis were murdering the Jews and burning their bodies.

Before the deportations, I was a little blond, blue-eyed boy without an armband to whom nobody paid attention on the streets. Once the deportations started, I wasn't allowed to run around outside anymore. I was confined to the apartment, where I began to feel like a caged animal. Once the deportations began, our parents hid Sabina and me instead of taking us out to show our documents. For some reason, we had a steel door on our apartment and my father managed to put padlocks and a crossbeam across the door on the outside to make it seem as if the apartment was locked up and empty. My parents hid us under the beds when the Nazis came with rifles, knocking and trying to get in. Eventually, they would give up, especially in the beginning, when there were still lots of people to catch.

Later on, as fewer people were left in the ghetto, the Germans had three big *Aktionen*, roundups, to weed out those who were hiding. They always chose Jewish holidays to close off all the streets and force everyone to come down to show their documents. We called those blockades *kocioł* in Polish, which means, interestingly, both "boiler" and "encirclement." It was then that our parents began hiding us in the attic of our building. The caretaker, a Jewish man appointed to that role by the Judenrat, helped to build a false wall in the attic under the sloping roof, where about thirty people could hide. When we were all inside, he shoved a big chest in front of it that had compartments in it to hold tools and oils. The Germans would come and look around and then leave when they couldn't find anyone. On one occasion, a small child cried out in the attic and a lot of people wanted to smother the child. That is a very painful memory.

After each *Aktion*, there was a lull for a few weeks and we could go back to our apartment, until the next one. One particular *Aktion* stands out because it was on Yom Kippur and all the men were hiding in the attic, praying. I don't know where my mother and sister were. The men were praying for deliverance and my father put his *tallis* over his head and mine and he was crying. He stood like that for a while, with his head and mine under his *tallis*, and the emotion of that is rooted so strongly in my being that today when I pray on Yom Kippur, that's where I am, standing in the attic in the Warsaw ghetto. At one point, I heard gunshots and got out from under his *tallis* and went over to the outside wall to look at the street through the slits in the wood slats. I saw that the Germans had closed off the street, and I could see the Ukrainian and German SS hurrying people along ulica Mila and shooting at them, and the Jewish police stacking all the dead bodies up like logs of wood. There was machine-gun fire going off for a long time; I can still hear it ringing in my ears. There were times when I couldn't believe that what I was seeing was real — this was one of those times. I felt I was looking into a surreal world.

We existed that way, by hiding, until April 19, 1943, *Erev Pesach*, the eve of Passover, which was also the eve of the uprising of the Warsaw ghetto. That day, there was an alarm. The few telephones that existed in the ghetto were still somehow working — these were mostly in apartments where doctors or other people deemed important lived — and the Polish underground resistance on the outside who were working with the Jewish underground phoned someone in the ghetto to say that the Nazis were coming in to take everybody out. By that time, there were already lots of bunkers in the ghetto. We had also prepared a bunker underneath the ruins at the front of our building. The caretaker and the men in our building, including my father, had dug it out, creating a middle section as an entrance and a room on either side. They didn't want to give up and be taken by the Germans and so they put in food, electricity and water and air vents so the bunker couldn't be discerned from the outside. My father and mother prepared us children for when we would have to go there. They told us that when the time came to go into the bunker, we were to ask no questions and we must get ready as quickly as we could.

That day, we all went down to the bunker, about 150 people in all. Something very touching that happened that day, and it has become part of my connection to my mother. It was early in the morning, about five o'clock or so, when our parents woke us up. My mother was holding *wełniane rajstopy*, woollen tights, which children wore in Poland in the winter, and she put two pairs of these tights on each of us. God forbid, she must have been thinking, that her children should catch cold.

My father must have brought wine, somebody else had matzos, and that evening in the bunker, they made a seder. Everyone was crying and praying. These were religious Jews who knew by heart the Haggadah, the Jewish text that sets forth the order of the Passover seder, and it still amazes me that, at such a dire time, they never forgot their culture and their morals. They also always made sure to shelter and look after their children.

I took my book, *Gone with the Wind*, which I had been reading for a while, with me to the bunker and I read it front to back many times. There must have been light in the bunker, as well as a trap door that could be opened so we could go out for some fresh air, but only at night, when the Nazis usually didn't operate. Even so, we had to be careful when we went out because there were informers who would come at night, mix with people and beg them to be let into their bunkers. That's how they found out where the bunkers were and the next day they would go and tell the Germans, who would come with flame throwers and artillery and announce that if the people didn't come out in half an hour, they would burn the bunker down. Eventually, the Germans levelled the whole ghetto that way.

We were in the bunker for about three weeks, and for the last few days we stayed inside and didn't venture out. People spoke only in hushed tones, which had a hint of hysteria in them. Then, the first week in May, the inevitable knock came on the trap door and we heard voices through the air vents. We had been found out. The voices — I can't recall if in German or Polish — said that if we didn't come out within half an hour, they were going to throw gas bombs into the bunker and we would all die. When we emerged, we saw Germans squatting with machine guns and they set the building on fire anyway.

One image has stayed clearly in my mind: As we left the bunker, we saw German paratroopers dressed all in black, like the devil himself, with black helmets and machine guns strapped across their chests. They kept shouting, "Hände hoch! Hände hoch! Nicht schiessen!" (Hands up! Hands up! Don't shoot!) They thought that we had guns and they were afraid of us. I felt very proud.

We were all searched and then forced to lie down next to the building, where Ukrainians guarded us. Now the collaborators were either Ukrainians, Latvians or Lithuanians. We stayed that way for a long time while they gathered up a large column of people. By the time we started walking, it was dark and we were surrounded by burning buildings. People were trying to escape, running away from the column, and one man ran toward the flames of a burning building as one of the guards aimed his rifle and shot after him. The guard was laughing himself silly as he shot, not even seeming to care whether he hit the man or not since it really didn't matter whether the man died of a bullet or in the flames.

That image became my first recurring nightmare; for years I would dream that I was being shot in the back and was dying as I ran into the flames. I seldom have this nightmare now, thank God. There were other nightmares later on, after 1955, when a different part of my brain kicked in and my real problems began, but that one was the worst.

The Ukrainian guards walked us to the *Umschlagplatz*, the round-up square for deportation. Then they forced us up some steps of a building into a room on the second or third floor of what had been an old Jewish hospital or Jewish school. That was the waiting station, the anteroom to hell. The room was small and they pushed as many people as possible into it so there was only space to squat. We all stayed that way the whole of that first night; it was a nightmare. People were in panic mode and the children were screaming and yelling all night while the Ukrainians pulled young girls out to rape. No one was allowed out, there was no food and the Ukrainians would give someone water only if he or she had gold or other valuables to buy it with. My father took my mother's gold wedding ring off her finger — I suppose that was all they had left by then — and bought some water. He had a sock with some sugar and a teaspoon in it, which he must have saved from the bunker, and my sister and I were given a teaspoon of sugar and a bit of water now and then. My parents didn't touch it, saving it for us.

Then we were chased out of that building. As we were running down the stairs and all the way to a train of cattle wagons, there were guards, Ukrainians and Germans, lined up on every second stair and standing all along the way with their barking dogs. They beat us with rifle butts, clubs, wooden planks and sticks. Once we got to the trains, they pushed as many people as possible into the wagons so you could only stand, but somehow my father manoeuvred us into a spot where we had some air. As he had always been, he was our guardian angel, his wings protecting his family. He was not a physically strong man, and he was a broken man by this time, but he obviously had a great deal of spiritual and moral resilience, because he did everything in his power to save his family. The fact that he had kept us so safe for such a long time is quite remarkable.

Into the Abyss

I was bewildered, in a state of disbelief, and what I most remember about the journey to Majdanek is that people — adults, children, healthy, sick, old — were in despair. People died in those wagons. Even under those conditions, though, people were helping each other, taking care of the children and the elderly. If someone was dying, they made a little room for them on the floor. Some people tried to break holes in the high windows for air and others cut the floorboards so they could jump out.

We were sure we were going to Treblinka, and if we had I wouldn't have been able to write this memoir because almost everyone died at Treblinka. But by this point in 1943, the Germans were losing the war and they needed slave labour, so they took some people to Majdanek to work instead. We arrived in Majdanek the first week of May 1943. When we got off the train, we were led into a large field and selections, where people were separated — men from women, children from parents — began right away. My father instructed me to go with him, with the men, and to say, when asked, that I was five years older than I actually was. He must have understood that young children were going to be killed because they were often too weak to work. I was tall for my age so the Germans believed me when I said I was sixteen. His advice saved me, and besides, I'm a religious Jew and I believe in Providence.

I was standing with my father when, suddenly, I saw my sister. She was standing with the children and then she saw my mother standing with the women and she ran to her. That was the last time I saw my mother and my sister. From that moment on, I forgot everything I ever knew about my sister. That boy who walked around the Warsaw ghetto with his eyes like lenses and his mind the film that recorded everything and could, if it were possible, make you see all the scenes he saw there — that boy forgot everything about his sister. This man, with his photographic memory of almost everything and everybody he ever came across, has forgotten how his sister looked. When I think about Sabina, all I can see is her blond braid with the ribbon in it. I cannot remember anything about her from before the war. We lived in the same room as small children, slept together, played, quarrelled, smiled and were happy. We lived in that little room together for almost three years in the Warsaw ghetto. I remember so many details about our family life before the war but I have only snippets of memory about her. I remember that my sister had beautiful blond hair that she wore in braids and that she had magnificent ribbons for her hair. But nothing else. I can't conjure up her face. I can't conjure up her body or other physical markers. All I can see is her back and her blond braid. I suppose I have blanked out everything about her and about what I felt when she was killed; even to this day, it is difficult for me to talk about her. There was only one time, when I was in Theresienstadt near the end of the war, that I suddenly started crying and when someone asked me why I responded that it was because my sister had died. But she had died in 1943 in Majdanek, and this was 1945.

After standing in that field for quite a while, the Germans chased the men into a barracks, where there were tables in the middle of the room. We were ordered to strip naked and throw all our clothes into a wooden bin. Then we were instructed to run, holding our hands high over our heads, toward a man with a white coat, an SS doctor, who was directing everyone and pushing people to the right or the left. I found out later he was sending people either to immediate death or to life in the camp. I was pushed to the right and then we were running, running, and the Germans were shouting, "Schnell! Schnell!" (Fast! Fast!) My father was running in front of me and I came into a room where I was thrown into a huge vat built into the floor that was divided into two parts and filled with strong disinfectant. If you didn't submerge your head, the kapo would knock you over the head and hit you until you went under completely. When I came out of that vat, every orifice in my body was on fire. Then we were forced into another room with showers and I thought, well, I might as well say my prayers and wait for the gas to come. But water came out instead and that washed the chemical off a little and made it burn a little less. We weren't given anything to dry off with before we were sent running to another barracks where prisoners were dishing out striped prison clothes with numbers on them and clogs. Then we were pushed outside at another end into the camp itself.

Once I got outside, my father wasn't in front of me anymore. As I looked for him, I saw the man with the boils whom my father had brought to sleep in our kitchen in the ghetto. I went up to him and said, "I'm looking for my father. Have you seen my father?" He didn't say a word; he just lifted his head to heaven. And I realized that my father had been murdered. I knew it immediately.

That was the first week of May 1943. I was not yet eleven years old when my mother, my sister and my father were murdered on the same day, the day that we all arrived in Majdanek. My father was thirty-eight years old, my mother thirty-five and my sister almost eleven.

I cried a bit when I realized they were all gone, but for a long time I couldn't really understand that they were gone forever; I only really accepted that they were dead after the war. Until then, I suppose I was hoping that they had been taken somewhere else, to another camp maybe, and were still alive. To this day, I still struggle with the reason I cried. Did I cry because I lost my father? Did I cry because I didn't die? I'll never resolve that question. I would like to think that I cried because I lost my parents and not because I was alive.

From that moment on, life became a matter of survival. My survival instincts kicked in and it was like I put blinkers on and did what I had to do to survive. Also, as a child, my brain was not sophisticated enough to look back. I was living in a kind of cocoon. I didn't have a past to draw on and was developing as I went along. I had learned in the ghetto to live from day to day and from minute to minute. You get into a kind of rhythm where you don't look right or left; you focus only on the minute. That is your existence, your reality. All that matters is staying alive. That skill helped me survive in the extreme moments, but unfortunately, in the long run, it has had detrimental effects.

Majdanek was very, very clean because the concentration camp commander was extremely particular. We were given a long harangue on cleanliness and what would happen if we weren't clean: We would, of course, be punished and everybody knew that, for the slightest infraction, you could be sent to the gas chamber. We didn't know there were gas chambers when we first arrived on the field in Majdanek, but as soon as I talked with other people, they told me what was going on there. Within a few hours of my arrival, I knew exactly what was happening.

I will never forget my first morning at Majdanek. When I woke up, I saw three young people hanging from a rafter. I assumed that they had committed suicide to avoid being sent to the gas chambers. Each barracks had a *Blockältester*, block elder or supervisor, who was in charge of the barracks, and he had one or two kapos. The kapos were mostly German criminals who had been sent there to serve their time; they wore armbands that said kapo on them and had regular clothes instead of the striped clothing of the Jewish prisoners. Our *Blockältester* was sadistic. I was told that, at night, the *Blockältester* and kapos got drunk and went into the barracks looking for young, good-looking boys to sodomize. Even after I heard that, I didn't realize what it meant. I was an innocent Hasidic boy who didn't know about sex, let alone that something like sodomy even existed. It wasn't until much, much later that I understood that the *Blockältester* was a violent pedophile who would have his way with these boys, choke them to death and then have them hanged. Then, at the roll call the next morning, the kapos would take the bodies outside and say they had died of natural causes or committed suicide. Even though I didn't understand exactly what was going on at the time, I knew I had to keep out of the way of the *Blockältester*. I lay in my bunk at night shivering, praying I wouldn't be next.

We were woken up at dawn and made to do exercises, a sort of calisthenics, where we had to jump up and down. We wore round, striped hats which they made us put on and take off, "Mütze an" and "Mütze ab," over and over again. This was part of a game they played, and they were very good at playing games with us. Whenever an SS man came around, we had to take our hats off to them like soldiers do in the army. When we finished our rituals, the kapo hurried us up to get outside for the *Appell*, the roll call, where we would sometimes stand for hours until they counted everyone and had selections, looking for people who were weak or sick to send to the gas chambers.

At the *Appell*, the Germans also assigned people to work groups. As always, they played games with this, too, in order to confuse us. They would sometimes say they needed electricians or plumbers for *Arbeitskommandos*, work groups, and when people stepped forward, they would send them to the gas chamber instead. Other inmates suggested not to step out when they called for people to be part of a work detail because you never knew if you were actually being called to work or being taken to the gas chamber. Even if you weren't sent to the gas chamber, the work details could be deadly. The Ukrainian guards took the prisoners out and used them to do hard labour for which machines were needed; for example, men were harnessed together to push the heavy rollers to compact the earth. Today, if you go to Majdanek, you can still see the rollers there. The guards beat people to make them work harder and harder and always brought dead people back at the end of the day. As I mentioned, it was a matter of survival to be as inconspicuous as possible. To be visible meant someone would notice you and something bad would happen to you.

At the entrance and on the side of our barracks was a little patch of garden with flowers and whitewashed stones, and when the guards were shouting and allocating work details, I decided to make myself busy fiddling with the flowers and the stones as if I had been ordered to work there in the garden. When the *Blockältester* would come and ask me what I was doing, I would say the kapo had asked me to clean the garden patch; if the kapo asked me, I would say the *Blockältester* had asked me to do it. I don't know how I knew to do that, or why. I somehow knew, automatically, that it could help me.

In Majdanek I was in a kind of cloud. We were always in the shadow of the gas chamber and that obliterated any other thoughts from our minds. I was always concerned with whether or not I was going to be selected for the gas chamber or selected to go to a work group and always thinking of how to get out of either option.

My existence in that camp is, I suppose, something I want to bury deep in my mind. Unfortunately, I cannot forget the salient points. One particular day, when I was lying on the ground making myself busy, fiddling with the flowers and the stones, a kapo whom I had never seen before approached and asked me what I was doing. I remember exactly what he looked like and what he was wearing: a three-quarter-length jacket, his hands in the side pockets, britches like riding pants, and shiny high boots. I told him that the *Blockältester* had ordered me to look after the garden and clean around it. I was lying there with my backside up, like an animal, trying to make myself invisible and then, without a word, he began to kick my back with his pointed boot. He kicked me hard, many times, and then walked away. I was in pain, bleeding. I still suffer from that beating to this day.

After I had been in Majdanek for about two or three months, one morning at *Appell* around the end of July, the guards asked for plumbers and electricians. Now, I knew it was dangerous to step out, but there I was, eleven years old, and I stepped out. Maybe my father was watching me from heaven — I always felt, in the ghetto and everywhere else, that my father was watching over me, just as he had, in the last minutes of his life, told me to say I was five years older than I was, which saved me. Quite a few other people stepped out with me. Who knows why they did — perhaps by that time they couldn't take it anymore and figured they might as well go to the gas chamber as endure this torture anymore. In any case, when enough people had been collected, we were taken to a barracks, where we had to undress. That was terrifying in itself because we knew what it meant when told to get naked — you were going to the gas chamber. Instead, a few men in white coats with stethoscopes came in and each one of us had to go over to them to be inspected. They thoroughly checked our lungs and hearts, and then sent people to either one side of the room or the other. Everyone on my side was to get dressed. I don't remember the exact sequence of what happened next but our striped clothes with the numbers on them were taken away and we were given different clothes, ordinary clothes and shoes, items obviously taken from dead people. Then the guards took us to the trains. They put us in cattle cars but this time they did not cram us in. We had room to sit on the floor and we were given food for the journey — a piece of sausage, cheese and some bread. Then we set off. We didn't know where we were going, but we were going.

A Terrible Existence

After a while, the train stopped. When the doors opened we were let out into an area surrounded by forest. Standing there were Ukrainian guards, SS soldiers and other men dressed in civilian clothes. Right away, the Ukrainians hit people and there was shooting. I think a few people died or were killed right there. Then some people were taken away while the rest of us were divided into groups and marched into a camp where Jewish police and Ukrainians were waiting for us. I would learn later that the Ukrainians were part of the *Werkschutz*, the factory security service, and were mainly the ones who guarded these camps, along with a few Germans. They wore black uniforms, carried rifles and were like any security force, except that they used to shoot and kill people.

The first thing I noticed was that a lot of people in the camp seemed yellow — their clothes were yellow, their hair was yellow and their skin was yellow. We didn't know where we were but found out soon enough that it was a working camp called Skarżysko-Kamienna and the work was in factories. The Polish government had built the factories there before the war and had needed the forests as camouflage because those factories were used to make anti-aircraft ammunition, bombs, mines and grenades. During the war, the factories were owned by the German arms manufacturing conglomerate HASAG (Hugo Schneider Aktiengesellschaft Metallwarenfabrik), in conjunction with some major banks, such as the Dresdner Bank. The Nazis had dozens of munitions factories like those at Skarżysko all across German-occupied Europe and used slave labour to make munitions and bombs for their war effort. The factories at Skarżysko are still there and in use today.

Skarżysko was made up of three camps, or *Werke* as they were called: *Werk* A, B and C. I was sent to Werk C, which was the worst camp in Skarżysko. It was the biggest one, with the most people in it, and the food rations were so small that starvation was a daily occurrence. The tempo of the work was unrelenting and continuous, day shifts and night shifts without pause, and the foremen, Polish gentiles and German supervisors and engineers, tried to have the work done as quickly as possible to reach the quotas the Nazis imposed. Most of them were cruel and their methods of trying to get people to work faster and faster were extremely harsh. If that wasn't bad enough, it was also the camp where people had to work with deadly chemicals like picric acid. It was this chemical that turned the people who worked with it yellow. This picric acid and the other toxic chemicals used were so dangerous that protective clothing was needed to work with them. The Poles and the Germans who worked in the factories had this protection, and masks as well, but the Jews had only the rags they were given, and the chemicals seeped through their skin and attacked their livers and lungs. If you were assigned to work in those *Hallen*, the buildings where they made ammunition with those chemicals, you were doomed. Between the scarcity of food, the unforgiving foremen and the deadly chemicals they worked with, people, depending on their constitutions, would die within a few months of coming to work in those *Hallen*. Thank God I was never anywhere near that work, but my cousin Michael arrived in Skarżysko's Werk C from the Lodz ghetto while I was there. I had been at his wedding in 1938 when he married my paternal cousin Terenya, the second-eldest daughter of my aunt Esther. They had already had a child when they were in the Lodz ghetto. His wife and child were murdered in either

Chełmno or Auschwitz, I'm not sure which; Michael didn't last three months in Werk C. I didn't see him there often but when I did, I noticed how swollen he was, and he died quite quickly.

As soon as we got there, we were assigned to work groups, each of which was headed by a Jewish policeman. Again, Providence was with me; I was assigned to a group led by a man called Katz. Our work was outside on the firing range, dismantling old ammunition, putting the gunpowder we extracted from it in boxes and then exploding the detonators. That first day, Katz asked all of us some questions and when he came to me, he asked where I was from. When I answered "Lodz," he said that he was from Lodz too and asked my name. He said that he knew the Gutter family from Lodz.

The next day, or the day after, Katz mentioned that his wife was ill and lying in the police barracks. These Jewish policemen lived in special barracks and were allowed to have their wives and families with them there. He told me that he wanted me to take care of her. I suppose he had made sure I was assigned to the day shift; he informed me that when I came back from my day's work, I was to go to the police barracks and look after her. For doing that, he would make sure I got some extra food. He kept his promise. When he was dishing out the soup, he would give me a ladleful from the bottom, where there was usually more substance as opposed to the top, where there was only watery liquid, and he also gave me an extra piece of bread. Katz's wife was dying of tuberculosis and I became her nurse. I washed her and cleaned her when she soiled herself and did whatever she needed. She lasted for about five or six months, and even after his wife died, Katz continued to be nice to me. I was never moved from his work group to any other even though the authorities were always moving people from one work group to another as needed.

The internal administration of the camp was made up entirely of the Jewish prisoners who had been at Skarżysko for a long time and had come from the surrounding towns and countryside. When these prisoners were brought to the camp, they had been able to bring items in with them. They then became the *Prominente,* the elite and intelligentsia of the camp; they had more privileges than the rest of us, like separate barracks and more to eat, and some even managed to somehow get hold of food and were cooking and selling it. Obviously, they had money hidden somewhere and were bartering with the Ukrainians and the Poles or smuggling things in from people they knew on the outside from before the war. People were searched on arrival at the camp, their belongings taken away, but there were always those who had ways and means, as in the Warsaw ghetto. The majority of us were starving, and then there was an upper crust of people who knew how to take care of themselves. Their lives seemed like paradise to us because they had plenty of food and other things and they had family members with them. The rest of the prisoners felt an enormous amount of anger and jealousy against these people but I didn't really feel this myself. At that point, I wasn't thinking in terms of good or bad. I was imprisoned in my own mind, only thinking of surviving from one minute to the next. I knew only that I had to cling to Katz, who was good to me. But even I saw how brutal the other Jewish policemen were, and Katz too, and how they would hit people with clubs and rubber truncheons without any thought or remorse.

The head of the internal administration of Werk C was a Jewish woman by the name of Fela Markowiczowa. She was the only woman who had a commandant position in the camp, and she had developed relationships with the factory management and camp authorities. She knew how to bribe the Germans and the Ukrainians to allow her to rule the administration of the camp as she saw fit. She put her family into positions of power, appointing one brother-in-law as the commander of the Jewish police, and another in charge of supplies. I know her mother was at the camp as well and given many privileges. The family had a barracks all to themselves and she held court there.

Markowiczowa was not a nice woman. She was part of the destruction machine, the machine of death, and distributed all jobs for payment or by whim, ruling with an iron fist and going around with a whip that she had no problem using. She came from a Hasidic family and before the war she had been a teacher in a Hasidic school, but nothing in Skarżysko was black and white. Today one can intellectualize and say these people were only trying to survive and did what they could to save themselves and their families. But it is difficult to rationalize the way that the Jewish police and administration treated their fellow Jews. People suffered terribly and saw that others of their own kind were not suffering as they did and had a better lifestyle at their expense.

One Jewish policeman, Calel Perechodnik, wrote a diary during the war. He was part of the Jewish police in the Otwock ghetto. Perechodnik died during the Warsaw Uprising in 1944 at the age of twenty-seven. His writings were published as his memoir long after the war, in the 1990s, and it is horrific to read how tormented this man was. He was not such a bad man, but he did awful things and couldn't forgive himself. He brought his own wife and only daughter to the deportation square because the Germans had promised him that his family would be safe, but the Nazis betrayed him and his family was sent straight to Treblinka, where they were murdered.

There were some Jewish policemen who really enjoyed their work and being cruel. There was one Jewish policeman who was in charge of the *Umschlagplatz*, the deportation square in Warsaw, and he collaborated not only to save his own life but also because he liked the position of power that it gave him. I read about him after the war and he was a psychopath, a terrible individual. When someone came to him and begged him to save them or their child, he would say, "Don't ask me to help you. I have a job to run this place according to the rules and that's what I'm going to do." At the *Umschlagplatz* there was a kind of medical clinic that the Germans set up with Jewish nurses and doctors. I suppose they were trying to fool people into thinking they were going to be taken care of. There was even an ambulance that could go in and out of the *Umschlagplatz* with no trouble, and the man from the Judenrat in charge of it tried to save children and others by smuggling them out. But this Jewish policeman did everything in his power to stop him in the cruellest possible way.

It is true that the Jewish police had to deliver a certain number of people a day to the Nazis or else their own families would be taken, and it is true that they were promised their families would be saved if they collaborated. But the irony is that, in the end, their families were murdered anyway; and I think that they should have known that. My father never trusted the Germans at all, even with all the documents he got from Rav Krol. After the war, when Nazis were asked at their trials why, since they gave their word of honour, they had lied to the Jews, some said, "Giving your word to a Jew didn't matter because Jews don't count. They are vermin. It's different if I give my word to someone else. Giving your word to a Jew means nothing." How could a Jew have agreed to be a policeman and trust the murderers of his people?

~

There were many women in Skarżysko, in separate barracks, some of whom the Nazis used to do the dangerous work of screwing the explosives onto the two-centimetre anti-aircraft ammunition because women had more delicate fingers. On Sundays, when we didn't usually work and had free time, there were opportunities for men and women prisoners to get together. But, as I've mentioned, men and women together did not register on me because I came from such a sheltered Hasidic home. If I saw girls and boys walking together and talking, it never occurred to me that anything but friendship was going on. Some of these women must also have had Polish boyfriends or even German ones, which didn't always work in their favour. It has been documented that some of the German foremen used to have parties where they would bring Jewish girls in and then shoot them afterwards because being with Jewish women was against the rules and they didn't want any witnesses.

The manic nature of life in the camp had no limits. Despite the horror and death and cruelty all around us, Markowiczowa did allow the prisoners to engage in some cultural activities and even supported the intellectuals and artists at Skarżysko. Men and women would sing in concerts that were held in the camp and we were allowed to observe the *Yamim Tovim,* the High Holidays, while the authorities and the Jewish policemen looked the other way. There were also many small acts of resistance. As in the Warsaw ghetto, lots of life-affirming events were going on while, at the same time, we were dying like flies.

There was an infirmary at Skarżysko, a *Krankenstube,* but everyone knew not to go there if they were sick. If you went to the infirmary, there was no guarantee you would come out alive. The nurses or doctors in the infirmary were Jewish and for the most part absolutely awful. They didn't have much medication, and whatever supplies they did have were yours only if you had something of value you could barter or bribe them with. Unless you were local and had connections with the Poles, who could smuggle things into the camp, you didn't get much help at the infirmary. The male nurses worked closely with the Ukrainian guards, and from time to time, trucks would arrive and take all of those in the infirmary who they felt were no longer useful into the forest to be shot. But the Nazis were always clever about this: The trucks would never stick to a routine and never came on the same day or time or even every week, so you never knew when they would show up or if they had already been to the infirmary the day or week you went looking for help. Knowing what happened to those who hoped for aid at the infirmary, people went to work even if they were deathly ill.

The outside work I did on the firing range was much better than being inside the building with the chemicals but still we were all on the edge of death due to the hard work, disease and starvation. If we didn't die on our own but looked really weak, the selections, which were often every few weeks, got rid of us. People who couldn't work anymore were taken to the forest to the open pits, murdered there and their bodies burned. Every night, trucks would come and take partisans, political prisoners and others to the pits, which we used to call *patelnia,* the Polish word for frying pan, because of all the smoke and the fire. The pits were on the other side of the forest from the firing range where I worked and we couldn't see the pits from there or what they were doing, but we did see the smoke and fire from the burning bodies.

It was a horrific camp in other ways too. Unlike Majdanek, it was filthy. We were full of lice and even though the authorities took us for disinfection once a month, they didn't give us new clothes afterwards; as soon as we put on our old clothes and went back to the barracks where the straw in the bunks was also infested with lice, the lice came back in no time. There was a Jewish woman in charge of the storehouse but she wouldn't give out new clothes unless you had some money or something of value to give her. Otherwise, you went without. Most people went without. Eventually, you would also lose your shoes, one way or another, but you weren't given new ones to replace them so we used the empty cement and chemicals sacks as shoes and secured the sacks with wire to keep them on. That's how we walked, even in the winter snow.

I saw a lot in Skarżysko that I have never spoken about. I can't talk about everything. There is so much that I experienced there and this is only one example. Our barracks were built on stilts, not right on the ground, so the latrines were outside, like outhouses. There were built-up rows of them where people sat next to each other, and underneath them there was all this muck running out into pits on the open ground. There were so many people, and we had to do our business so quickly, that a lot of the sewage collected in huge pools around the latrines. The pools of feces were large enough that people committed suicide by jumping into them. These poor people were skin and bones and they knew their days were numbered, so rather than be shot, they jumped into these pools of feces. How do you end your suffering in a place like that? People found ways.

Inevitably, from time to time, someone was chosen to clean up that sewage. Katz may have been my policeman but that didn't stop somebody else from grabbing me and saying that today I was going to do that. You had no choice; you had to do what they told you. I don't talk about this because it's so despicable to talk about. One cannot imagine what I see in my mind's eye when I think of that river of disgusting sewage flowing. It has left its mark and made me very conscious of cleanliness to this day. I rarely use public washrooms and I am hyper-conscious of my hygiene. That is one of the loose ends left over from my life in Skarżysko.

It was a terrible existence but you had to find ways of surviving, of staying alive from moment to moment. One thing that kept me alive was my relationship with Katz. I was luckier than most because Katz made my life slightly better. He would tell me where the leftovers outside the police or administration barracks were placed after they ate so I knew where to go and scavenge scraps of food like peels from potatoes and other vegetables. I would bring these back to my barracks to share with my best friend, Yaakov, who was several years older than me. We looked after each other. In a camp, if you didn't have a close friend or somebody older than you who had more understanding, you were lost. I would share everything with Yaakov. That's how we tried to help each other survive.

For many, though, life was a losing battle. When too many slave workers died, the Germans needed new ones and brought people in from camps such as Plaszow and Auschwitz. After the war, I read that it wasn't so easy for the Nazis to keep up the supply of slave labourers coming into the work camps to restock the ones who were dying and being murdered, yet somehow they managed. But in November 1943, when the people from Plaszow came, they brought typhoid with them. I caught it. I didn't want to go to the infirmary because I knew that if I did, there was a chance I wouldn't come back. So I went to work sick and my friends hauled me to the firing range and dragged me back every day. With this type of typhoid there is one crisis day when you get a very high fever, and if you break through the fever, there is a chance you might survive. That day, I was so sick I couldn't even walk. There was no way I could make it to work. My friends put me on a top bunk in the barracks and covered me with straw. "With God's help," they said, "they won't see you there and take you to the infirmary."

Every day, after the work details had left, the Jewish policemen would come to the barracks to make sure they were empty and that everyone had gone to work. They always brought with them a Ukrainian with a rifle to add incentive for those who weren't willing or able to go to work. The day I was lying there in the top bunk, a Jewish policeman and a Ukrainian guard came to inspect my barracks. It was my luck that the Ukrainian waited at the door. Maybe he wasn't too keen on going inside because of the typhoid epidemic. The Jewish policeman came in and checked every row of bunks, standing on the bottom one and looking up into the two bunks above. At my row, he stepped up onto the bottom bunk and looked straight up into my eyes. Then he shouted, "Keiner da!" (Nobody's there!) and walked back to the door. They both left, closing the door behind them. That Jewish policeman risked his own life by saving mine that day. Providence.

The next day — either again because of Providence or because of Katz — I was switched to the night shift to work inside with the Jewish women, supplying them with the sacks of black powder to put into the bullets they were making. The women knew I was ill and saw how young I was and they took care of me. They told me not to do any work, to sit and recover instead, and they gave me a signal to begin work when one of the foremen was coming, especially the cruel Jewish foreman whom we called *der grosse Avram*, big Avram; everyone was afraid of him. I would stop again and rest as soon as the foreman left.

One experience I will never forget is that one of the women brought me an apple. I don't know where she got it — an apple was unheard of, and I had never even had one in the Warsaw ghetto. To get an apple in a concentration camp was incredible. She simply approached me and said, "Here, Pinek, have an apple." I ate the apple and you can't even imagine the way that apple tasted to me. I have never forgotten this. To this day, apples are the fruit I like best because of one apple that a Jewish woman gave me in Skarżysko.

Food was always an issue in Skarżysko. The official rations were as follows: In the morning we got what they called coffee — it was made out of acorns or leaves perhaps, and it looked like dirty water but we drank it anyways because it was hot. At lunchtime we got soup, and depending on how much the Jewish policeman liked you, you either got from the top, which was mainly water or from the bottom where, if you were lucky, you got a bit of horsemeat or some rotten potatoes or beets as well. In the evenings, the Ukrainians would bring in bread from the bakery, and no matter what the rations were, they would sell some of the bread on the way to the barracks. So, depending on how much bread there was when they got to you or who and how decent the Ukrainians were, you never knew how big a piece of bread you were going to get. One day they would divide each loaf by eight and the next day it could be divided by twelve, depending on who was cutting it. I think we got another soup or coffee in the evening. In spite of the little bit of extra bread or thicker soup I would get from Katz, I was skeletal. Even Katz couldn't fatten me up.

In January 1944, the food situation improved a little. The Nazis couldn't replace people the way they had in earlier years and realized the Jews they had were all the Jews they were going to get. In November 1943, the SS had gone on a killing spree. After the uprising in the Sobibór camp, as well as in other places, Himmler decided that it was time to execute the "Final Solution" and he devised a plan to kill all the Jews in the SS-administered camps of the Lublin district of Poland, specifically in the concentration camp of Majdanek and the forced labour camps of Trawniki and Poniatowa. *Aktion Erntefest*, Operation Harvest Festival, was the code name the Germans gave to this operation. On November 3, 1943, the operation began at dawn and by the end of the next day, approximately 42,000 Jews had been murdered.

But all the factory camps like ours were officially under the administration of the Wehrmacht, not the SS, since HASAG paid the SS in Radom five złoty per day for each male labourer and four złoty a day for every woman. The Wehrmacht needed us and didn't want us killed, so we were protected from that *Aktion*. However, this slaughter made it impossible for the Nazi authorities to give our camp any more Jews and a commission was sent to our camp to see how they could improve our rations so we could work harder and longer. After that, a loaf of bread was divided into only four portions and the soup was much better. The rations improved not because they wanted to help us but because without us they couldn't supply the army with the ammunition they so desperately needed. By then, the Poles were mostly gone, some taken to Germany to work and the others in hiding or having gone to the partisans. They needed Jews.

When I recovered from typhoid, I was switched back to the day shift. Katz must have arranged it so that I would mostly work with him, which I did until the end of July, on *erev* Tisha B'Av, 1944. The Germans often used the dates of Jewish holidays to commit terror. As an aside, I am often asked how we knew when the holidays were and what date it was in general. Hasidic and religious Jews in the camps counted the days and knew exactly when the holidays were. In my barracks there were two religious men, one named Friedman and the other Kamjonka, a man I knew from the Warsaw ghetto. In the evenings, after curfew when the lights went out, Kamjonka would stand by the window with a little Talmud and study or pray by the light of the moon, and he was able to keep track of the days and months. It's amazing how religious people kept their faith in the camp. Markowiczowa allowed them this since, as bad as she was, she came from a Hasidic family, so I suppose she had some feeling for the rabbis and religious people. Both these men survived the war and became rabbis.

On July 31, 1944, after we returned from work, Katz told us that we couldn't go straight back to the barracks. Instead, we had to go and see Commander Schulze, the Nazi commander of Werk C. Schulze was an Austrian police officer and a terrible person. He had lost his arm in World War I and we called him *Hantke,* little hand, because he had a wooden arm. Whenever anyone said, "Hantke," we knew we had to look busy or make ourselves invisible.

That day, he sat at the window in his office and we all had to walk by him and give him our names. As we did, he marked a tick beside each name. When everybody had gone past his window, they took us back to the barracks and gave us whatever food we were entitled to.

The next morning, we did not go to work. An *Appell* was called. SS guards with machine guns surrounded the camp. Commander Schulze appeared and announced that the camp was being evacuated and we were all going to a new camp. Those whose names were called would be going by train but since there weren't enough train cars for everybody, those whose names were not called would have to walk there. Then he started calling out names. I heard the name of my best friend, Yaakov, and then mine; we both went to the area where the others whose names had been called were and stood there side by side.

There was a woman doctor working in the infirmary who was good friends with Schulze, always walking around the camp with him. Prisoners had mentioned to me that she took care of the medical needs of the Ukrainian families. Her mother was in the camp with her and when Schulze called out her mother's name but not her own, she ran to him, grabbed his sleeve and begged him to go with her mother. He continued what he was doing, not paying any attention to her, but she wouldn't let go of his sleeve. The next thing we knew, he had taken out his revolver and shot the mother. Then he shot the doctor.

Those of us who had been told to stand aside noticed that all the people with us were the ones who looked yellow and were wearing rags like Yaakov and I were. We soon realized this was a selection for the forest, not a train ride to a new camp. We started running. I saw a chest on the ground, where dead bodies were kept until enough were collected to be taken out of the camp and disposed of in the forest. I jumped into that chest but was so terrified in there with the dead bodies that I leapt back out, crawled under the barracks and burrowed myself into the ground like an animal. For years after the war, I didn't know if I remembered this incident correctly. Was there really such a chest or had I been so traumatized that I had envisioned it? My memory was confirmed when, after the war, I read the book *Death Comes in Yellow* by Felicja Karay, who writes about this chest.

Once everyone was running, the SS, the Ukrainians and the Jewish police were ordered to round us all up for a new *Appell*. Katz found me under the barracks and said that he would help me. He took me to the police barracks and had me take off all my rags, including my paper-and-wire shoes. He then washed me and combed my hair, and applied one of his wife's old lipsticks onto my cheeks to give me colour. Then he gave me a complete set of proper clothes, including high boots like the police wore, a jacket and a hat. As he sent me out he said, "Schulze is going to have another selection and he's got about five hundred names on his list to kill. He's going to find that five hundred people regardless of who is on that list. That's how they work. Maybe, with God's help, you will survive."

I went back out and got into the line, which was now being heavily guarded. Nobody wanted to be at the front of the line, where it would be easy for them to be picked out, so the older prisoners pushed the youngsters to the front. I was standing in the front row beside my friend Yaakov who was still wearing his rags, just like the ones I had been wearing earlier. Then Schulze went from row to row and pulled people out. Those people were ordered to go to the other side, where they were surrounded and heavily guarded by Jewish police and Ukrainian guards. When he came to us, he walked past Yaakov and stopped in front of me. I was shivering and so afraid that he would remember me, or that he didn't like me for some reason. He looked at me for what seemed like an eternity and I was sure he was going to take me out. But then he grabbed Yaakov, pulled him out of line and pushed him toward a policeman who came and took him. Then he continued on. I watched in horror as they pushed Yaakov into the circle with all the condemned men. When they had their quota of five hundred, they took all those prisoners away to their deaths.

After the *Appell,* the rest of us were taken to the trains. I have read that a total of 6,500 prisoners were evacuated from Skarżysko that day. As for Yaakov, I grieved that boy for years and years. I grieved for him more than I did for my own family. I had nightmares about him and couldn't get over the fact that he was my *korban*, the sacrificial lamb who had been taken in my place and murdered instead of me.

~

After the war, I learned that Markowiczowa, who was wealthy and on good terms with the Ukrainian guards and the Nazis as well, had found out that the camp would be evacuated on August 1, 1944. She decided to free herself and her family the night before by bribing Schulze, the commander. Some of the Jewish policemen and others in the administration found out what she was planning and threatened that if she didn't include them in the escape, they would tell everyone of her plan and she wouldn't get out either. At two in the morning, the Ukrainian guards abandoned their stations, allowing Markowiczowa and those fleeing with her to cut huge holes in the barbed wire so they could all escape. As they all ran into the forest, the guards reappeared and began shooting. Markowiczowa had been betrayed. Of the 250 or more who tried to escape, most were caught and killed, including Markowiczowa herself. Katz, too, was one of those who died that night.

Some did manage to get away into the forests, where they were then killed by Polish partisans, but one of the people who survived was Markowiczowa's mother. She was a decent person and whenever anyone in the camp was in trouble with the police, she would intercede on their behalf. That night, the mother ran to the forest and found a farmer she knew from before the war, who saved her. Perhaps she survived because of all the good she had done. After the war, there was a huge immigration of Jews to Paris; someone from Skarżysko saw Markowiczowa's mother on the street and she recounted the story of how she survived.

Becoming a Man

We were shipped out of Skarżysko in train cars to a town called Częstochowa, where there were several working camps that also belonged to HASAG. I ended up in Żelazna Huta, which was an iron smelting factory. This camp seemed like a sanatorium compared to Skarżysko. We never saw a German inside the camp and only one person ever died in that camp when I was there — and he was a youngster who was not careful. The camp was beside railway tracks on which there were trains going by night and day, taking tanks and ammunition to fight against the Soviet Union and coming back with wounded soldiers from the front. This boy must have gotten too close to the rails and one of the guards shot him. Because we had been surrounded by death for so long, had seen it so intimately, we thought we had somehow become immune to its power. The enormity of death had almost become a normal, everyday occurrence. But when that one boy died in Częstochowa, it was extremely traumatic. Somehow it was more traumatic than being surrounded by hundreds of dead bodies in Skarżysko and later at Buchenwald. One single individual dying was a tragedy.

The greatest difference between this camp and the other camps I had been in was that the *Lagerältester*, a Jewish commander, was a kind and wonderful man. I think his name was Frankel but I can't be sure. He chose decent people to be kapos and went out of his way to help the children. When one of the young boys had appendicitis, he arranged for the boy to be taken to a hospital in Częstochowa for the operation and then to actually be brought back. He also had the tailor in the camp cut up blankets and make jackets for the kids so we would be warm in the winter. I also still had the clothes and boots that Katz had given me, so I was well protected that winter.

There were three categories of work in this camp: light, medium and heavy; depending on what kind of work we did, we were given a metal tag for a particular amount of food. The system was such that the harder we worked, the more food we got. Frankel arranged it so that the youngsters got medium tags no matter what work we did. The food wasn't nearly as bad as in Skarżysko either and even better than in any other camp I had been in. The work I did was with a group in the steel-making factory. The molten steel was poured into moulds and then we threw water on the ingots to cool them off. Then we had to take heavy ingots out of their moulds and load them on the rail cars. We had to work quickly because there was a quota of how many ingots we had to produce and load in a day.

In Częstochowa we suffered from the hard, heavy work and also from being slaves to the Germans, but not from the treatment we received from the Jewish administration. As a matter of fact, I used to call this camp *Beit Havra'ah,* the Hebrew word for a sanatorium, a health spa. I had warm clothing for the winter, we got decent food, we weren't full of lice, and I'm sure that my stay there gave me the time to heal and the strength to survive what came after we left there.

When I arrived at the camp, I found Rav Godel Eisner, a great Talmudist who had been a friend of my father's since they had studied in the same yeshiva together. One day, Rav Eisner came to me and said, "I was at your brit milah [circumcision], and now that you are turning thirteen, we're going to make you a bar mitzvah." By that time I had lost all hope and long neglected any religious observances. I didn't want to go through with it and was afraid of the possible consequences. Even though this camp was more flexible and not so strict, it was an extremely dangerous undertaking. There were constant

Appells and we were closely watched. No matter how kind some of the guards might be, we knew we were risking death. Besides, I felt no religious need for it; I told Rabbi Eisner that I didn't want a bar mitzvah, and I began avoiding him from that day on. I tried to keep out of his way but he persisted until I finally agreed.

Rav Eisner was not in my barracks so on the night we arranged for the bar mitzvah, I exchanged places with a person from his barracks — he came to sleep in my bunk right before curfew and I went to his barracks for my bar mitzvah. I hid under his bunk until all was quiet and then we proceeded quickly. Even though any type of religious observance was strictly forbidden in the camps, religious Jews managed to find ways to continue to practise their faith. I don't know how, but they managed to smuggle all kinds of things in; Rav Eisner had managed to smuggle *tefillin*, the black leather box and straps that Jewish men wear to pray, and a Siddur, the Jewish prayer book. He put on the *tefillin* and gathered ten men for a *minyan*, the number needed for a traditional service. I repeated the *brachot,* the benedictions, after him and then the *minyan* prayed together. When it was done, he *benched* me, blessed me, and said a few times in Yiddish, "Mit got's hilf vest du iberlebn Hitler." (With God's help, you will survive Hitler.)

In spite of myself, I was caught up in the fervour of the event and it renewed my hope that I might actually, with God's help, survive. I believe that having my bar mitzvah in that camp really did help me survive. It gave me strength. Years later, an American woman named Arnine Cumsky Weiss found out that I had my bar mitzvah in Częstochowa and approached me to share my story when she was writing a book about unusual bar mitzvahs. My story is in her book, *Becoming a Bar Mitzvah.*

I was in Częstochowa for a few months, I think from about August to December 1944. Then the Soviets were approaching, and by November or December, we could hear the fighting at the front. The Nazis evacuated us prisoners and we were shipped out again. They put us into rail cars but for the first few days the wagons didn't move.

We just sat there on the rails. The cars were open and there were no locomotives or guards. They gave us some food and left us there. If we wanted, we could have gotten off, but where would we go? We knew the local population wasn't going to help us. So we stayed in the rail cars and were there outside the camp on a siding for two or three days while other trains kept coming by, including Red Cross trains with wounded Hungarian and Romanian soldiers. We youngsters would run across the rails and beg them for food, which they gave us.

After a few days, a locomotive arrived, as did a troop of SS guards. They closed the wagons and the train moved on. I don't know how long we travelled, but when we arrived on the siding outside what we didn't know at the time was Buchenwald concentration camp, there were guards with dogs waiting for us. As we were herded off the train, the guards were shouting, "Schneller, Schneller!" (Faster, Faster!)

No one who wasn't there can possibly imagine what Buchenwald was like at the beginning of 1945. It was pandemonium. Soon after we arrived in the camp, the German gentile kapos of the internal administration asked us who the bad policemen or kapos in our previous camp were and then told us we should "deal" with them. So people did that. There were those who, I suppose, had grudges against the man I called Frankel, the *Lagerältester* from Żelazna Huta, because when they found him, they beat him to death and threw him into a pile of other dead bodies. While they were beating him, there was no way that anyone could help him — if they had, they would have been next. I was devastated when I learned that he had been murdered. To me, he was a humane man. He ran the camp in such a way that we didn't have to worry that any second someone was going to kill us. We worked hard but he guarded us and helped us. I found out later from other people who came before me that *der grosse Avram* was also murdered in Buchenwald. Although he had treated people so badly, I don't believe he should have been murdered.

As soon as we arrived, the German kapos interviewed us and asked us strange questions like what childhood diseases we'd had. We were all assigned a certificate, a *Häftlings-Personal-Karte*, and mine, which was issued on January 20, 1945, a copy of which I obtained after the war, says that I had been arrested because I was a *Politische-Pole-Jude,* a political Polish Jew. I was a political prisoner then, not an innocent child enslaved simply because I was a Jew.

We were placed in quarantine with about one thousand people, crowded together in a barracks, and given almost no food. Prior to our arrival, criminals had run the camp administration, but by the time we arrived, it was being run by the German communist prisoners. They were obviously still under SS rule but I think the SS wanted to be on their good side — they must have known that the end of the war was coming and that they would have some explaining to do. There were satellite work camps at Buchenwald but by this time not everyone was working because of all the chaos. The communist administration tried to keep the atmosphere sane but we were living like rats. It was the most horrible camp you could imagine. Everyone was trying to stay alive by grabbing life from everybody else. Since it was the end of the war, there was hardly any food and people were dying from hunger and disease. Each morning there must have been between forty and fifty bodies of people who had died during their sleep. The living were counted; the dead were taken to the crematorium.

I can't recall how long I was in Buchenwald, but one day names were being called out and if yours was called, you had to go to the clock tower at the entrance of the camp. Everyone knew that going to the tower was ominous — the SS were either going to execute you or find some other means of torturing you. On that occasion, people who had come from Częstochowa were being called out, me among them, and we all went to the tower. Then suddenly, along with some others, I was on a train again. We didn't know it at the time and only found out later that HASAG had been looking for us. They needed us to work.

We were shipped to Colditz, famous for its castle. We didn't arrive at a camp so much as a factory, where huge halls had been converted and outfitted with bunks for workers. The commander of the camp was a middle-aged SS man, like most of the SS men there. I suppose that all the young ones were fighting at the front. The commander wasn't even an officer; he was an *Oberscharführer*, a senior sergeant. He looked us over and said, in German, that all the youngsters must step out. Of course, no one wanted to step out. Youngsters couldn't work as hard and we all knew what that meant. But when he called for youngsters to step out, I was the only one who did. I don't know why, but again, something or someone must have been guarding me, either Providence or my father.

When the group was dismissed, the *Oberscharführer* took me by the hand and led me to the SS kitchen. When he told me I would be working there I could hardly believe my luck. Working in the kitchen meant only one thing — food. But the commander didn't send me to the kitchen because of his good heart — he had an ulterior motive. He had a bag with him that he hid in the corner; he explained that no one could know about it and that every chance I got, I was to put some potatoes or other food in it for him. Then he would come at night and take the bag. The next morning, the bag would be back in its hiding place, empty and waiting for me to fill it up again. We both knew that if I got caught, I would be shot, but I nevertheless did as I was supposed to. Thank God, I was never caught.

As I worked in the kitchen, peeling carrots, I ate some and after dinner, when I was cleaning the vats, I would eat the little bits of meat that were left at the bottom. I didn't throw any of it out. It just so happened that Rav Godel Eisner had also been sent to Colditz, and we met there again. He had been shipped directly to one of the factories in Schlieben from Częstochowa and our train, I suppose, was to have gone there too but had been sent to Buchenwald by mistake. So, in the evenings, after I had eaten my fill in the kitchen, I would give Rav Eisner my ration of bread and soup. He survived the war and I met him again in Paris when he was on his way from Poland to Israel. I know that he became the head of a yeshiva, remarried, had a family and lived well into his nineties. It feels good to know that, while he was in Colditz, I was able to give him my bread and soup in the evenings. That's how it works, God's Providence. The Rav made my bar mitzvah in a dangerous and unlikely place and when I found him later, I was able to give him some extra food to help him stay alive.

We were in Colditz for several months, until the middle of April 1945. One morning, we found out that the camp was being evacuated. We were each given bread, some sausage and cheese and ordered to march. By early evening, we were in a forest in Germany when one of the SS guards, a *Volksdeutscher* corporal who spoke Polish, told us that we were free and that they were going to take off their uniforms because the Americans were coming. Everyone went crazy and started eating whatever food they had left because we were all so hungry. Suddenly, a troop of SS arrived and shot into the air. They made us lie down with our faces in the earth and said that anybody who raised their head would be shot. We lay there all night and by the next morning we were marching again. So much for freedom.

We were literally starving to death as we marched along, day after day, and as we walked through the German towns, the residents threw stones at us, abused us and refused us any food or water. Every night the guards would push us into barns and they counted us every morning to find out how many of us had died or run away in the night. They were unwavering in their resolve to find the runaways, even at this late stage, and see to it that, if we died, it was with a bullet to the head. Sometimes when we slept in a barn we would eat the raw grain we found. If we were lucky enough to find a pump, we would have some fresh water to drink. If we didn't find anything, we would drink the dirty rainwater from the ditches and eat leaves and grass from the sides of the roads. We became so desperate that some people even ate insects to stay alive.

One night, when we were staying in a barn, we were so exhausted and so hungry that we ate the raw corn or wheat or whatever was being stored there and then all collapsed for the night. The next morning when the SS counted us, one person was missing. There was, among us, one young man who was the darling of the guards. He was about twenty years old and good-looking, with freckles and reddish-blond hair, and I have no idea how he managed it, but he was always well-dressed. During the count, it was discovered that this young man was the one missing. They counted again and again and then we had to stand where we were, not moving, until he was found. Eventually they did find him, asleep under one of the sacks of grain. He had been so exhausted and so starved that he had not heard the call to get up. When the SS collected him, a middle-aged corporal put this young man's head between his legs, took out his revolver, which had a wooden handle, and shot him in the head at close range. Then he left him lying there on the ground, mutilated and still trembling, and one of the prisoners went over and took his shoes off. The SS had adored him, and yet they shot him only for oversleeping.

This event is still so vivid for me and I cannot forget that incident or that young man's face when he was alive. The shock of what happened to him was engraved indelibly on my mind. How does one deal with these things? It is the one thing that I have never been able to reconcile. In normal times, one takes for granted the cycle of life and death, but slaughtering men, women and children by the thousands and dying without dignity or respect is not normal. You had to fight against it, push it away from your consciousness, if you were to remain sane and, even more importantly, human. For me, at that time, death was anything but a normal life progression. After the war, I started living in a normal environment, but my consciousness and my mind had been constructed and corrupted in the camps and I was not able to see death as part of the human process. My life had been put on a particular path during those five years of camps and ghettos. My fears and attitudes were moulded and pre-determined by those years and it is nearly impossible to undo what was done to me.

On the other hand, I did encounter the occasional glimmer of humanity. We were constantly being warned that anyone who straggled behind the group would be shot but it was hard for many of us to keep up since we were all so tired, hungry and weak. The SS *Oberscharführer* who had taken me to the kitchen was leading the march, travelling up and down the column of people on an ordinary bicycle, and whenever I started to lag behind, he would pull up beside me, put his hand on my back and push me back into the column, telling me that I must keep up and march. He would actually put his hand on my back and gently push me back into the crowd of marchers. As we marched along, the guards would shoot animals or rob farmers for food, which they would eat on the go, and this same *Oberscharführer* would occasionally give me a bone. He did help me.

Halfway through the march, right before we crossed into Czechoslovakia, a high-ranking SS officer came along on a motorbike, stopped the column, put his bike on its stand and stood up on the saddle to speak to us. He told us that there was to be no more killing. "You are all comrades," he said, "and must help each other. If someone is weak and can't walk, four people must carry him." He gave instructions to the guards that there was to be no more shooting, then got back onto the motorbike and drove off. Everyone began to talk about him, speculating who he was. Some said he was an angel from heaven while others thought he was a partisan dressed up as an SS officer. Still others said maybe the Germans had changed their minds and decided to stop killing Jews. In the end, it didn't really matter. Whoever he was, the guards obeyed his orders and there was no more shooting, although people still died after that from weakness or starvation. Of the approximately 1,500 people who started out on that march, I think only half arrived at our final destination —Theresienstadt.

Finding Life Again

When we crossed the border from Germany into Czechoslovakia, people threw food to us from their windows. In the German towns, they could see we were concentration camp Jews because we were so bedraggled and half-dead but they had thrown stones at us and vilified us. Yet in Czechoslovakia, people threw food to us. When they did, the SS would shoot into the air and tell the Czechs to stop throwing food or they would shoot into their windows.

We walked for about two and a half weeks without knowing where we would end up as we marched along. By the time they marched us into Theresienstadt at the end of April, I was close to starvation and collapsed in front of a column of people. Somebody came and gave me a piece of bread and a piece of sausage; it was the first real food I had eaten in two and a half weeks.

A week or two later, we were liberated by the Soviet army. I remember the day of liberation quite vividly. In the morning, the first thing that we noticed was that the Czech gendarmes and German guards had disappeared; then, Soviet frontline soldiers, mainly Tatars and Uzbeks, started coming through the gates. After a while, we all rushed out and I found myself with a band of youth who were wandering around. We soon came to the main highway and saw a multitude of German refugees trudging along, either being expelled from Czechoslovakia or fleeing back to Germany. There were mainly families with children carrying *pekalekh*, bundles, and walking with wheelbarrows or riding in horse-drawn wagons or on bicycles. As they walked along, they were being assaulted by Czechs, mainly, and some Soviet soldiers and a few survivors, too. I remember very clearly my own sentiments of pity and commiseration toward these German refugees because they reminded me of my own suffering and the suffering of my family. Some of my companions also expressed similar sentiments. Even after all these years, I still find it intriguing that instead of the intense hatred I should have felt toward these people because they were German, what I felt was empathy.

As I was walking beside a field, I noticed a pair of horses hitched to a wagon, grazing. Nobody else was around so I stayed with these two horses, fascinated, and forgot about everything else. I sat on the ground and watched them, reminded of when I had played with the horses on my grandfather's farm. After a while, I plucked up my courage, climbed onto the wagon and picked up the reins. "Wio!'" (Go!) I shouted in Polish, just as I remembered wagon drivers doing before the war. And the horses responded and started moving.

Once I drove the horses into Theresienstadt, they became mine. Theresienstadt had become a camp for those of us who had nowhere else to go, and though I had a bed there, I spent most of my nights sleeping with my horses in the barn I created for them in a broken-down building. They became my family and I was very attached to them. As I had no food allocations for them, I had to scavenge for whatever I could find, like stale bread, which I soaked in water, and hay, which I cut from the ditches and dried in the sun. The horses did not do too well on this diet and had diarrhea until I finally found a sympathetic Soviet field kitchen sergeant from whom I begged some oats so I could modify the horses' diet.

I began to work for the Soviet and Czech administration of the camp, using my horses and wagon to deliver food to the German prisoners-of-war and SS soldiers who were being held for trial as war criminals. One day, as usual, I delivered the food from the camp kitchen and the man in charge of giving it out told me he was in need of an assistant. He asked if I would stay and help serve the food. I wasn't too keen on this. The German prisoners, anxious to get to the food, began pushing, yelling and clamouring for their portions, which made me so angry that I lashed out and threw a ladleful of food at them. Afterwards, I felt tremendous remorse. In my mind, I had become just like the Nazis, like the cruel and heartless men who had treated us so badly when we were starving.

I felt empty at the end of the war. I was a loner, an introspective person who walked the streets by myself in a fog, like I had in the Warsaw ghetto. I was disenchanted with the world and I did not feel like getting involved with other people. I mostly kept to myself.

There are days, still, when I can hardly believe I survived all of it. I ask myself, how was it possible for anybody to survive Skarżysko? According to statistics, approximately 25,000 Jews went through that camp and about five thousand survived. I can only say, once again, that it was Providence. I don't know if I would have survived Skarżysko if I hadn't had Katz to watch out for me and if he hadn't had a wife who was ill so I could look after her. And then there was the SS kitchen in Colditz where I worked and had enough food for myself so I was able to give my rations to Rav Eisner. And the *Oberscharführer* on the bike during the death march who pushed me back into the column whenever I lagged behind. But, even with the help of Providence, how did I make it? I think in part it was because I worked at making myself invisible. Like a horse with blinkers on, I didn't look right or left, didn't catch anyone's eye. I merely existed in that maelstrom of iniquity and tried to hide inside myself so I wouldn't be part of it.

The writer Aharon Appelfeld, himself a child survivor, said in *Encounter,* a book of essays on his writings, that for young people, the five years of the Shoah — the ghettos and the camps — that was their upbringing. These children didn't have a past and they didn't know about a future. The Holocaust wasn't a normal life, but it was the only life they knew. I was one of those children. I grew up in abnormality and the Shoah taught me to be a survivor. It was my education, and its cruelty and death, with the occasional flicker of good fortune, was the only normal I knew.

~

After the war, the UNRRA, the United Nations Relief and Rehabilitation Administration, decided to sponsor a program that would see Britain take in and rehabilitate about one thousand Holocaust orphans. On their behalf, British philanthropist Leonard Goldsmid-Montefiore persuaded his government to agree to a special scheme whereby young orphaned survivors would be flown to Britain, put up in hostels and trained for a new life. Eventually, 732 children made the journey to Britain and were resettled throughout the UK.

I was among the first group of 350 orphans chosen to be on the first flight to England but when the time came for me to leave Theresienstadt, I refused to go unless I could take my horses with me. I had become so attached to my horses, the only family I had left, that I refused to leave them behind. There were many tears on my part when I was told by a Czech official that I couldn't take them with me, but he was kind and clever and said that although horses couldn't fly on planes, if I would agree to go on the plane to Britain, he would have the horses sent to me by boat. I agreed, but of course, once I got on the plane, I never saw my horses again.

We flew to Prague first, where the squadron of RAF bombers were stationed that would take us on to Britain. While in Prague, we were housed with Catholic nuns who were part of the Caritas Society, an arm of the Catholic Charities. The nuns took care of us and showed us the sights of their beautiful city. Years later, I led a group of Catholic educators from the College of Saint Elizabeth in New Jersey on a tour of Holocaust sites in Poland, and they in turn invited me to come and speak at their college. When I went there in 2006, they presented me with the Order of Caritas and gave me a bronze plaque for distinguished service. Ironically, after being looked after by the nuns of

Caritas in Prague after the war, years later, I was given a plaque for my own services by this same organization.

On August 14, 1945, ten converted RAF Stirling bombers flew us from Prague to the RAF base at Crosby-on-Eden, near Carlisle in England. They put thirty to forty of us into each of the bellies of the planes where the bombs used to be and we flew to our new homes. "The Boys," as we were called, were taken to Troutbeck Bridge, a tiny hamlet near Windermere in the Lake District of England. During the war, a training camp for officers had been built there, and this camp had all the facilities we needed — buildings with bedrooms, sports facilities, huge halls for dining, classrooms and a gymnasium for indoor sports. It was a ready-made camp for rehabilitation.

The British government had specified that the orphans brought over should be sixteen years old or younger but a lot of the "children" were actually not children at all; they were seventeen or eighteen years old. After we settled in, the head of the Jewish refugee organization told us that everyone must give their true date of birth to the authorities because they were getting us organized for classes to resume our education. I was only fourteen at the time but quite tall, and when the official asked my date of birth, I replied that it was what I had given them, July 21, 1932. Truthfully, I only knew my birthday in Hebrew, the 21st of Tammuz, and either I or someone else had made a mistake and put July 6 instead of July 21 as my birthday. I also didn't remember at the time that, in the German document from Buchenwald, the year of my birth was listed as July 21, 1927, because my father had, from the beginning, told me to say I was five years older than I really was. The official got cross with me, not believing that I was only fourteen. He decided to punish me for lying and put me in the class with the younger children.

I wasn't happy and I felt discriminated against, but I did my best to participate in the life of the camp as we swam, went on hikes and played sports. I was also part of a club called the Primrose. Decades later, in 1963, the members of that club formed a group that we called the '45 Aid Society; we collected money and gave it once a year to worthy causes. We still keep in touch to this day and have reunions yearly. We also publish an annual journal before Rosh Hashanah called *45Aid Journal*. In this journal we write stories about what happened to us in the war and encourage other people who were in camps, not only "The Boys," to submit their stories. I myself have written the story of my bar mitzvah, and others as well.

Two occurrences stand out for me in my three months at Trout-beck Bridge. The first had to do with my curious nature — I like to know and I like to learn. We had a nurse at the facility but no hospital and if someone was ill or needed dental work, they were taken to the hospital in Windermere. I often saw a big Rolls-Royce drive up to take kids to the hospital and I was fascinated by the car. I have always loved motorcars and thought it would be lovely to have a ride in this Rolls-Royce. But how would I get to ride in that car? I went to the nurse and lied that I had a toothache. The next day or so, the Rolls-Royce arrived and took me to the dentist who asked me where the toothache was. I pointed to a tooth and before I could say another word, he strapped me in and pulled out my perfectly healthy tooth. I have never replaced that tooth, so as to remind myself to not let my curiosity get the better of my good judgment.

The second incident involved my battle with sports. Coming from a religious family, I had never played any sports whatsoever but the sports director tried to get me to play soccer, which is called football in England. I had what we call in Yiddish, *tsvey linke hent un tsvey linke fis*, two left hands and two left feet, meaning that I was clumsy, and I had no idea how to go about it. Since I was strong, my team put me in goal, and although I had fantasies of flying up and catching the ball, I didn't catch any at all. The other boys on the team were older and they made fun of me and kicked the ball at me to ridicule me. The sports director saw that soccer wasn't going to work out and decided that, since I was a big, stocky boy, I'd be a good candidate for boxing. I put on the boxing gloves and stepped into the ring where my opponent was waiting. He was a few centimetres shorter than I was and much skinnier but the next thing I knew, I was on the floor and unconscious. He gave me one hit and that was the end of my boxing career. It was also the end of my sports career at Windermere — it was apparent to everyone that I wasn't a sportsman.

For a long time after the war, I didn't think about what had happened to me in the Holocaust. I thought only about being alive, and I acted in the moment, in the present. Although I didn't have any problems or nightmares for the first ten years, I suffered from the lack of being a social person. I wasn't an active part of the group and am not even in any of the photographs taken of the Windermere children at that time. I wasn't a sportsman or socially active, and because of that, I was always kind of pushed aside by the other boys. We were at an age when boys and girls became aware of each other and a lot of the boys and girls were friends at Windermere but I wasn't friends with any of the girls either. I was there with 350-odd girls and boys, but I spent a lot of time alone and again was isolated, living mainly in my own brain and with my own thoughts. That didn't do me much good then or later on in life.

I think that my solitary nature had a lot to do with how safe I had felt with my parents, who provided my sister and me with a carefully monitored environment. Even in the ghetto, my parents guarded us fiercely and we spent much of our time alone, in hiding. In Skarżysko I had my friend Yaakov, but other than that I was never part of a group. I was always solitary — both in my intellectual and my social life. So Windermere, even though it was really quite a wonderful experience, merely accentuated my differences from the other kids.

Fortunately for me, Rabbi Weiss, the rabbi who was in charge of our religious activities, knew of my family and my grandfather and he took me under his wing. He saw that I did not really fit in at Windermere and decided that I should go to a yeshiva hostel called Etz Chaim in Whitechapel, in the east end of London. They called them "hostels," which is a much nicer word than "orphanages," but an orphanage it was. Again, though, it was difficult for me there. The boys were much older there, too, and quite nasty, as boys can be. They abused me by forcing me to do things I didn't want to do and beating me up if I didn't.

I spent close to nine months there and hated every minute of it. In fact, I was so unhappy that, eventually, I ran away. We were allowed to take a weekend off from the yeshiva and I did just that and went to stay at a hostel in Ascot, where I knew some boys were staying. I complained to Mr. Heinz, the social worker there, about my treatment at the yeshiva and my unhappiness. A German who had come to England before the war, Heinz was a wonderful man. He told me I didn't have to stay at the yeshiva and said that if I didn't want to go back, I could remain in Ascot and he would have my clothes sent over.

But even in Ascot, I was unhappy. Again, I didn't fit in. The boys were much older than I was and paid little attention to me. They all had non-Jewish girlfriends, and although a few of the boys tried to pair me off with a girl, I was too innocent and it was very awkward for me.

One incident from my time there shows how isolated and rejected I felt. I liked to go to the cinema, and the rule at Ascot was that if you went to the five o'clock show, supper would be left for you when you got back. Once, after I had been to the cinema with some other boys, we came back to find the table set with supper for everyone but me. I may not have been social, but I was quite assertive and also strong. I got so angry and frustrated that I lifted the long, heavy table up so all the plates of food on it went flying.

After that, Heinz decided there was something wrong with me and sent me to the Great Ormond Street Hospital, which specialized in children's issues, to be checked over. I went once or twice and the psychiatrists gave me all kinds of tests, like the Rorschach. At my final checkup a doctor concluded there was nothing wrong with me. She said that I simply liked to assert myself and preferred to be independent, on my own, and there was nothing the matter with that. She suggested I go to the ORT (Organization for Rehabilitation through Training) trade school where I could learn how to be an electrician or a carpenter. I went for a short time, quickly realizing that I didn't want that either. I decided that what I wanted was to live with a family and go to work. Everyone — Heinz and the Jewish relief organization, called the Central British Fund — agreed that I would be happier in that kind of environment and they found me the Diamond family in Crouch End, north London, who agreed to take me in. I paid them for board and lodging, but they became like family to me. I shared a room with a young man named Victor and the two of us spent lots of time together. He became a lifelong friend.

From then on, I had very little to do with the boys with whom I had come to England. I went on a few outings with the Primrose Club before we formed the '45 Aid Society, but not many. Instead, during the week, I went to work and on Saturday mornings, I went to shul with the Diamonds; often, in the afternoons, we would go to the beach at Brighton together.

I started off my working life potting plants in an English gentleman's house. The lord of the house was always on horseback. I don't think I ever saw him walking. One day, I was in the shed potting flowers when he came in. He asked what I was doing and when I responded, he said I wasn't doing a good enough job, that I wasn't doing my best. I guess my temper got the better of me — I pulled off my apron and angrily said that if my best wasn't enough for him, he could have his plants and his job back. Then I walked out.

My second job was as an apprentice at the Ford Motor Company. Since I loved motorcars, I thought this would be ideal, but one of the jobs an apprentice did was to dismantle all the parts from army surplus vehicles and clean them up so the mechanics could use the parts in putting together second-hand trucks for sale. The engine blocks were always used because they were in fine condition and then new spark plugs were put in and other usable parts were reconditioned. My job was to unscrew the engines, wash them with paraffin and clean them. Doing this, I was having problems breathing. At the clinic in the factory, the doctor told me that the smell of the oils and cleaning materials was bad for my lungs since I had weak lungs due to my pneumonia as a child. He advised me to change jobs.

Next I was sent to work for an optician, where my apprenticeship consisted of sweeping the floor and making tea. I wasn't there long before the optician mentioned that his wife was ill and asked me to do him a favour by going to his home and making her some tea or whatever she needed. This in itself wasn't an issue, since I had been nurse to a sick woman in Skarżysko, but when I arrived at their home, I found they had two big dogs. Dogs were not my favourite animals, especially because the Nazis and their vicious dogs were still fresh in my memory. Also, in Hasidic homes, we did not have animals. The optician's wife was in bed when I came in. She asked me to make her tea and do some other chores around the house. Then she asked me to take the dogs some food and clean out their kennels. The kennels were full of garbage and I went back to her and told her I had come to her home to help out because she was ill, but I was not a servant and wouldn't look after her dogs. "I am an apprentice optician," I reminded her. I politely said goodbye and went back to the shop. I told my boss I couldn't clean out his dogs' kennels and he said that was fine, but that I couldn't work for him anymore.

The next job I found was in a factory that I think was called the Sigma Corporation. They made frames and lenses for eyeglasses and I worked as an apprentice there for quite a long time, in fact until I left England at the end of 1948.

My cousin Rav Krol was living in Paris when I came to England, and he discovered I had survived when he saw my name on a Red Cross list at the end of 1946. He came to England to see me and tried to persuade me to come to France. I didn't want to go to France — I was finally happy in England, working and living with the Diamonds — but he persisted and eventually I agreed to come for a visit. I wasn't a British citizen but I had British resident papers and that made me eligible for a special British document for travel. The French wouldn't give me a visa to France, but they would allow me to travel through France to Switzerland on a transit visa. So I went by train to the ferry and from the ferry onto another train that took me to Paris, where, instead of going on to Switzerland, I got off the train. The Krols were waiting for me at the train station. A few weeks after I arrived, I had to appear before a judge at the Prefecture of Police because I was in France illegally. The Krols prepped me on what to say, that I was a Holocaust orphan and my family wanted me to stay in France. The French treated refugees well at that time and they gave me a document that said I could stay for six months. When the six months were up, I got another document for three years. So I stayed.

I had really never had any residual problems from the Holocaust until I came to stay in Paris. At the Krols' home, I had a nightmare of being gassed in a gas chamber. Rav and Andja Krol's bedroom was next door to the room where I was sleeping and I must have screamed out in my sleep. They heard me, came in and took me into their bed. I was sixteen by then but they put me in the middle of their double bed, between the two of them, and it took a while before they could quiet me down.

The Krols had established a small textile factory outside Paris and Rav Krol, his wife, their daughter, Therese, and I lived above it. The factory had two mechanical looms making gabardine and three or four hand looms making woollen scarfs. A few Holocaust survivors worked there alongside a few French workers. The Krols sent me to learn French, and within a few weeks, I was fluent enough in colloquial French that there was no point in my continuing to go to school. I started working at the factory and ended up managing it. I would get up every morning at five, start up the furnace and wait for everyone to get there. I learned how to work the looms, how to make designs and about deliveries.

I worked there until I was eighteen years old, and at that point I decided I didn't want to live with the Krols anymore. I was disenchanted with my life there — I was a bit rebellious and I wanted to strike out on my own, to be my own man. The Krols had helped me but I felt like a stepchild to them and I had a sort of love-hate relationship with their daughter, Therese; maybe she saw me taking the place of a son that her parents never had. I don't know for sure. Our relationship wasn't volatile but it was slightly uncomfortable for me. Therese was very smart and later went on to become a professor. She is now a professor emeritus at the Hebrew University of Jerusalem, and she and I are friends today.

I decided that what I wanted was to go to Israel and join the army. I had wanted to go to Israel right after the war and had dreamt of becoming an officer but I didn't want to go as a refugee and I didn't realize that you couldn't become an officer without an education. At the end of 1951, I bought a ticket and went by ship to Israel to join the army.

Dorothy

When I arrived in Israel, the immigration official spoke to me in Yiddish, asking what I wanted to do in Israel. I told him I wanted to join the army and he said, "Listen, you live in France, where it is easier. Life is not good here — food is scarce, there is disease and it's too hot. It's hard to live here. Why don't you look around before you join the army to see if you really want to stay?" But I said, no, I want to join the army. He stared at me and remarked, "There are a lot of crazy people in the world and you are one of them." Then he informed me where to go to join the army.

I went through recruitment camp and boot camp and became an artillery sergeant in charge of transport. I was working very hard and was so thin that the medical doctor of my regiment called me into the clinic for a checkup and decided to send me to a health resort, a sanatorium in the hills of Haifa, to fatten me up. Otherwise, he told me, I was going to get tuberculosis. I was at the sanatorium for about ten days or two weeks and I went on hikes, made friends and got better food to eat. The doctor actually sent me to that sanatorium twice. I was in the army for the obligatory two and a half years and then they kept me on for another six months because they couldn't find anyone to replace me. I liked the army and was content with my work.

When I left the army, I worked as a manager of the Keter Textiles Factory. The owners were two Belgian Jews and I worked diligently for them and was earning a lot of money, but I wasn't happy there. I found them to be quite difficult to work for and we didn't see eye to eye, so after about eight or nine months, they paid me out and I left.

While I was working at the Keter Textiles Factory, sometime toward the end of 1954 or the beginning of 1955, I had my first incident relating to the Holocaust. Since the war ended, I had been relatively free from repercussions, except for that one nightmare in Paris, but that changed one Saturday afternoon in Israel. I was part of a group of Windermere boys who had also come to Israel to volunteer for the army and we formed a sort of little club. We were pretty close and got together either Friday nights or Saturdays to go out and eat together and talk. One of our favourite restaurants in Tel Aviv was a Hungarian restaurant where we liked the goulash. In those days in Israel, everything was closed on Shabbos, on Saturdays, and if you wanted to go to a restaurant on that day, you had to buy a ticket on Friday and then you could come to the restaurant on Saturday and they would give you a meal. We were at this Hungarian restaurant on one particular Saturday, sitting on high stools at the bar and talking, when I suddenly fainted and fell to the floor. It didn't take long before I came to and then I was okay. But that night, I had my second nightmare.

From then on, I was having nightmares more often, as well as health problems. I began having stomach issues and the doctors did a number of tests, even putting a tube into my stomach, but they couldn't find anything physically wrong with me. They told me I had low acid, the opposite of an ulcer, and gave me pills. Then I began having heart palpitations and back pain. The doctors x-rayed my kidneys and again found nothing wrong. I was busy going to doctors all the time but none of them could find anything physically wrong with me. In addition, I started getting panic attacks. I would be sitting in the cinema and part of the way through the movie I would start to panic and had to get out because I thought I was going to die. My issues were psychosomatic, but the symptoms wouldn't go away.

I decided to leave Tel Aviv and go to Jerusalem. I wanted to educate myself and signed up at the *ulpan* in Jerusalem to learn correct, grammatical Hebrew. I knew how to speak, read and write Hebrew, but I wanted to learn the language properly because I hoped one day to get my high school diploma. I had saved up enough money from working to study full-time and was at the *ulpan* for five months. It was there that I met Dvora, or Dorothy as she is called in English, and we started seeing each other. However, even when I was with Dorothy my panic attacks happened — they had followed me to Jerusalem. Dorothy was so kind and she coped with all of my problems with so much patience that I believe she was what saved my life.

Dorothy was a university graduate with a degree in literature and she was from South Africa, where her parents still lived. She had been born with a genetic hearing problem and there was only one doctor, in England, who did fenestration, a special operation to correct her condition. After we had been going together for about a year, her parents decided to send her to England to have the operation.

By then I had finished at the *ulpan* and was working again. I had several jobs, none of which satisfied me. My first was as a labourer on the site where Yad Vashem, Israel's memorial to the victims of the Holocaust, was being built on the western side of Mount Herzl. When the employment officer told me that he would get me a job as a steel fixer I admitted to him that I knew nothing about construction. He said not to worry, that I'd pick it up in no time, and gave me a note explaining my situation to the foreman. It took me only two days to figure out the work and I worked as a steel fixer for a while. Next, I worked for some time breaking stones for a company that was preparing the ground for planting trees, and after that as a laboratory technician making pills. However, none of these jobs really suited me.

I had been renting a room from a woman who was the chief librarian at Yad Vashem's Jerusalem office and she told me they needed a technical assistant at the library. So, as fate would have it, I worked in the library of Yad Vashem. But it was difficult work for me to do. My job was to photocopy European synagogue records from one hundred years earlier and translate documents and testimonies of survivors for the German and Czechoslovakian governments. In doing that, I had to relive my own experiences, which was quite hard for me. At the same time, I was trying to cope with my nightmares and physical ailments. I also missed Dorothy. We had been corresponding since she left and we both knew that we wanted to be together. We decided that I should come to England and we should get married. When the Sinai War, or the Suez Crisis, broke out on October 29, 1956, I was on standby but it ended so quickly that the army never called me up. When it was over, I began the process of leaving Israel. I got a release from the army and bought a plane ticket to join Dorothy in London.

In November 1956, soon after I arrived in London, Dorothy and I got married at the Registrar's Office. In the 1950s you couldn't live together before you were married, so we got married right away and rented a room from the Diamonds' eldest daughter, who was then a widow and rented out rooms in her house to make a living. Dorothy's brother was also in England and he rented an upstairs room there, too, and we shared a little kitchen.

On January 6, 1957, I borrowed Mr. Diamond's cylinder hat and Dorothy borrowed a hat from Mrs. Diamond and we had a proper Jewish wedding at the Finsbury Park Synagogue, where Mr. Diamond had been president. The Diamonds made us a high tea after the ceremony at their home and then Dorothy and I went to the cinema. That was our honeymoon. We consider that as our real wedding, and January 6 is the anniversary date that we always celebrate.

Once we were settled, I decided that I would pursue an education and I registered at the adult education school run by the University of London, where people from all over the world came to study. I chose to study full-time and not work since I had accumulated some savings and Dorothy was getting a monthly allowance from her parents. Together, we decided, we could manage. I was very good at history and languages but I needed physics, math and chemistry to get my diploma and I wasn't good at those. My history teacher was a white-haired gentleman with whom I became friendly. When he came to our flat one evening for supper, I admitted how worried I was about writing the exams in the sciences. He told me that I shouldn't worry too much about understanding the material. I had a photographic memory, he said, and if he gave me some books and old exam questions to look at, he was sure it would be easy for me to memorize the answers. I wrote the exams and did manage to get through all of them. I got high marks for all the humanities and miraculously succeeded in passing the sciences and maths in spite of the fact that I didn't understand the material; I don't understand it to this day. I received my diploma and knew that was all I could do.

By then, our money had started to run out and Dorothy was pregnant. We discussed what we would do now, and when Dorothy's uncle came to visit us from Brazil, he told us that we should come to Brazil because the gold was "lying on the streets and you only had to pick it up." So we decided to take our baby daughter, Tanya, who had been born in September 1957, and move to Brazil.

We arrived in Brazil in August 1958. I didn't like it there at all. When we got married, Dorothy's parents had wanted us to come to South Africa but I didn't want to go there because of apartheid. But Brazil, I discovered, wasn't much better. Everyone was equal under the constitution but in reality the country was run by a dictator, so the constitution was irrelevant — people of colour were considered second-class citizens and workers were treated like dirt. Dorothy's cousins lived like nobility and I, who was a nobody, made good money, lived like a king in a magnificent apartment and had a maid, a Japanese woman named Luzia, who had a separate little apartment next to ours and took care of Tanya.

When Dorothy became pregnant with our second child, she decided she wanted to go home to South Africa. Her doctor told her that if she wanted to travel to South Africa, she must go right away, before she was too far along in her pregnancy because, in those days, the only way to get there was by boat. In February 1959, Dorothy left Brazil with Tanya, who was only a little over a year old at the time. I wasn't able to get a visa in time to leave with them because the South African government, the National Party, was antisemitic and made it difficult for Jews to immigrate. If, however, you had a job waiting for you in South Africa, you could get permanent residence papers. Dorothy's family was well off and her father owned several small shipping companies in Cape Town. When he sent me an offer of a job as manager for one of his companies, I was able to apply for permanent residence in South Africa. To boost my chances, the British consul in São Paulo, who was friendly with the Jewish community, wrote to the South African immigration department on my behalf and recounted my history. He wrote a positive evaluation of me, really building me up, and tactfully left out the part about my having been in the Israeli army, which the South Africans wouldn't have looked upon favourably. I waited nervously for the papers to come through, afraid I would not be able to leave before our baby was due. Even though I had all the documents in place, I still had to wait until July before the paperwork was finalized and I could leave Brazil. Happily, I arrived in Cape Town eight days before our son, Jan, was born and was able to be in the hospital with Dorothy when he arrived. Rumi, our youngest child, was born in South Africa seven years later in 1966.

The Turning Point

When I got to South Africa, I started working for my father-in-law. We had an uneasy, tenuous relationship — he hadn't wanted us to get married in the first place and was upset that we had. Dorothy's parents hadn't even come to our wedding. I had met her mother in Israel when they came to visit Dorothy before we were married but her father hadn't wanted to meet me. He didn't want a Holocaust survivor as a son-in-law. After all, who was I? How was I going to make a living? How would it all work out?

I soon realized that my father-in-law didn't trust anybody and had no friends. Even though I was working diligently for him, his animosity and mistrust of me continued, and he didn't treat me well. He gave me such a low salary that I was constantly struggling to support my family. He had a penthouse in Cape Town on the top floor of the building he owned where his offices were and a big house on the water where they lived in the summer, but Dorothy and I and our children lived very poorly in a little apartment.

In 1961, about two years after I arrived in Cape Town, Dorothy's mother died and her father, who was quite handsome and dapper, became a real "ladies' man." It seemed as though women were always interested in him, and in 1967 he remarried. For their honeymoon, he and his new wife, Cecilia, went on an extended long boat voyage. I was left to look after some of the work process, but instead of putting me in charge, he brought in an accountant and made him managing director of the business. I was hurt by that. He knew I was unhappy about his decision and suggested that I get another job. Since he had only strangers working for him, I felt it my duty to stay on so my father-in-law had someone from the family around. His son, Elijah, had moved to England and didn't want to be a part of the business, and Dorothy and her sister, Rosalind, weren't going to get involved.

As soon as my father-in-law left, the accountant he put in charge began giving me a hard time because he actually wanted to take over the business and he saw me as a threat and obstacle to his plan. I managed as best I could since I knew that, as difficult as he was, my father-in-law was the only father I had and I needed that. When he was away on his honeymoon, that need built up in me and I was a wreck until he came home. However, when he came back from his honeymoon, he gave me an even harder time, which had devastating effects on me.

When Dorothy and I lived in England, my psychosomatic symptoms and panic attacks had abated. I had nightmares sometimes, but no more physical ailments. The same was true of the time I lived in Brazil. But when I moved to South Africa and started having problems with my wife's family, I began struggling emotionally again, and in 1967, I was having horrible nightmares and flashbacks. Instead of going to a doctor or a psychiatrist, though, I started drinking a little wine every evening when I came home. Soon I was going upstairs to my father-in-law's penthouse at lunchtime, where his cook made me lunch, and having a little sherry or another type of alcohol with the meal. I had never been a big drinker — I hated alcohol — but I was drinking as a way of calming myself down. It relaxed me and put me into a sort of void, but at least I could sleep. However, it soon became a problem.

Eventually, the accountant arranged to sell the business to a large company — he could see he wasn't going to be able to get rid of me so easily. I think my father-in-law realized then that I was the only person he could rely on, and after the company was sold in 1969, he wanted me to stay on as the manager for the new owners. I stayed with the new owners for three months and then I left. In 1970, my father-in-law and I created a new finance company, which ultimately was very successful.

But I was continuing to struggle with my emotional issues. I was again sleeping terribly and I now had the extra burden of trying to build up a new business while, at the same time, wanting to be there for my young family. The truth is that I wasn't always available to them — I was either working or struggling with my demons. I would come home, have a drink and go to bed. It was as much as I could cope with to be at work for eight hours. I had nothing left when I came home. At that time, I was just lost, and I didn't know how to get better. Today, people realize that post-traumatic stress disorder (PTSD) is an actual illness. Imagine the kind of PTS the Holocaust can have on a child. I know I can't relate to things emotionally the way other people do. I don't have the capacity, for example, to truly, deeply enjoy beauty. If I am on a hike, I cannot revel in my surroundings; I think only of the achievement of getting to the other side. If I am at the opera or the symphony, I always feel as though something is holding me back from appreciating the experience. It is as though I always need to be on guard — I am always wondering what is going to happen next. I feel this same way whether I am reading a book or seeing a film; it is like I am sitting on pins.

The children knew I was having difficulties — they could see it. They were growing up in a house where one parent was unwell. I was ill all the time. This was not easy for them and I am sure it affected them. Even though it was hard on them, they were always supportive of me, even when they were young. I wasn't a bad father — I was always very loving to my children — but my wife was the glue that kept us together. Dorothy, who is a wonderful person with a great intellect, really brought up the children. I wouldn't have blamed her if she had walked out on me then but she never gave up, and to her credit and my good fortune, she supported and helped me when I desperately needed support. I truly believe she is the main reason why I am here today.

Dorothy began urging me to see a psychiatrist and I took her advice. Once I found one, though, my issues became even tougher as I tried to work through my memories. I struggled to cope. I was depressed and anxious but I forced myself to get up every day and go to work because, at the same time as I was learning how to live with what had happened to me in the war, I had to make a living. The doctor gave me anti-depressants, which didn't make me feel right so I didn't take them, and then he switched me to anti-anxiety medications, which did help a little. Every day, I was reliving the horror of the Holocaust and then forcing myself back to the realities of my current life and the responsibilities of a man with a family. It was brutal for me, and my wife took on the brunt of the work at home. She was the one who looked after and educated the children and took care of the home. I worked and struggled to participate in our family life while trying to overcome the chasm that still existed between me and my father-in-law.

The crisis came in 1975. I was unable to continue living like I was, and I ended up spending a week in a nursing home. A clinical psychologist there became like a mother to me and she somehow helped me to discover where the problem lay. The psychiatrist I had been seeing in Cape Town was fine and had helped me, but this psychologist made the critical difference. I saw her for only ten days but she really made me see what was happening to me. She believed that my current problems arose from my struggles with my father-in-law, which had brought up all the other problems I had relating to the Holocaust. I had no parents and I hadn't had any since I was a young child. But my father-in-law was not what I needed a parent to be. She helped me realize that many people had parents who did not treat them well. My father-in-law was not such a nice person but he was, for all intents and purposes, my father. She talked me through it all and convinced me to see that what I had was a bad father, but I had to live with that. So what if I had a bad father? It was still better than no father at all.

What she said made sense to me and penetrated through my emotions. It made me look at my situation from a different point of view. When I came back to Cape Town, I continued to see my psychiatrist for quite a while but I was not feeling the same as I had been before I went to the nursing home. I had started analyzing my relationship with my father-in-law. I could see that he and I had a lot in common and came from similar backgrounds. He came from a shtetl in Lithuania and I was from Poland. We both spoke Yiddish. He had his own demons from a difficult childhood and I had mine. It wasn't his fault that he came from a difficult background. It shaped him. And it wasn't my fault that I came from a difficult past that had shaped me. I could now see that he relied on me more than on anyone else, even more than his own children, and that he identified with me more than with anyone else. When he got ill, he didn't want to see anyone except me. Once I came to terms with him, everything else began getting better. I stopped using alcohol and I stopped taking pills.

When I stopped seeing my psychiatrist professionally, we became friends and he confided in me that when I began my therapy, he was sure I would be in analysis forever. "You see that slit at the bottom of the door?" he asked me once. "Only a mouse could maybe get through that narrow slit. But you managed to do it. Now you are on the other side and you'll be fine." That was the turning point. It didn't mean that I stopped having flashbacks and nightmares after that, but it was clearly different from before. They didn't interfere with my life to the same extent. There were several times when I had a few relapses — days, each time, of horrendous difficulties — but, slowly, slowly, it got better. Issues in the mind take a long time to heal.

~

When I started to heal, I also started to come back to my beliefs. My religious beliefs had vacillated off and on in the years after the war. I hadn't been happy in the yeshiva in England, and in Israel I completely turned away from religion. My wife is not a religious person, and in South Africa I wasn't living in a community that fostered religious belief. My father-in-law and all the family there were not religious. They were traditional Jews but not observant and went to shul only for the High Holidays. Friday nights were special, but not in terms of religious observance. Once I was feeling better emotionally, I also became more traditional, though not Orthodox.

It was 1977, when I was forty-five years old, that I got involved with community work and in the Jewish community. I became a sort of community leader and I sat on various Jewish boards, worked with seniors and became a cantor. My community work gave me an injection of confidence.

We lived in South Africa from 1959 to 1985, but I never wanted or intended to stay there forever. Dorothy's brother had immigrated to Canada in 1967, and in 1977, I came to visit him in Toronto when I was in New York on business. I had never thought about living in Canada, but when I walked around the city, I felt such a freedom with every breath I took. It was the most humane place I'd ever been. This is a magnificent place to live, I thought, and decided we should move here. When I came home, I told Dorothy that we were going to move to Canada, to Toronto. But it took some time to get here. With my work, the children and family obligations, we finally were able to come in 1985.

Today, I regard Canada as my home. My true home will always be pre-war Poland but that is all inside of me. England was never my home even though I was happy there and it is where I met the Diamonds, who were like my own family, and I loved them. But Canada is my home. Canada gave me the opportunity to become truly involved in the Jewish community I lived in. It is one thing to get involved in a cause or a community but quite another to stay involved. I wanted to help people, and once I got involved in one area it sort of took off from there. I studied chaplaincy for two years so I could do services for those who were dying at long-term care facilities like

Baycrest Hospital, and for many years I was a chaplain at the Don Jail in Toronto. There weren't many Jewish prisoners and the most I ever had at one time was eighteen, but I conducted services there for the Jewish inmates twice a month and arranged kosher food for those who needed it. I have been involved in community work ever since 1977, giving of myself and to charity, from that day until today. I truly believe that it is this community work that has kept me going. It's cathartic and therapeutic, and it has given me more than I have ever given to others.

I think I'm a warm-hearted and caring person. Maybe I am like my father and grandfather. I hope so. Basically, I believe that it wasn't so much the war itself, but rather some of the good that happened to me during the war that has made me who I am. Maybe who I have become has to do with looking after Katz's wife when she was dying in Skarżysko, or the policeman who risked his own life and lied that there was no one in the bunker when I was sick with typhoid. Or the woman who gave me an apple and helped me recover. Or my bar mitzvah. I saw great evil during the war but I saw some humanity, too, and I could absorb this because I had seen these values in my own home and in the ghetto years in the way my father struggled to protect his family.

The seeds of all that I am today were actually planted before the war and during the war, in the times I was with my father and was shown the positive side of humanity. The day we were liberated and I saw the Germans being chased out, I felt sorry for them and had empathy for their plight. I knew what they were experiencing. I was only a child when I lost everything I loved. My journey has included great sadness and loss but it is founded in the goodness I saw in my childhood and in some moments of the greatest darkness of my life. I think my desire to stay involved with humanity and help where I can comes from the Aramaic saying *girsa d'yankusa*, what one learns in youth. A lot of who I am comes from what I learned in my youth.

Final Thoughts

The majority of people don't want to hate — they only want to raise their children and make a living. But for others, hatred blossoms and you can see the hidden loathing, the antisemitism that has been festering for years. Unfortunately, in some, it is alive and well. All people are capable of hating — hating Jews and hating Israel. But how do you make the world a better place? Only by teaching the children. Only through education can you teach people not to hate. It is not a matter of tolerance, as some people believe. You can teach people to tolerate but there also has to be acceptance — acceptance of individuality and diversity.

We are the children of light and the children of darkness. Through the ambiguities, we must try to see the positive. We have to understand that, in spite of our differences, basically we are all the same whether we are Jews, Muslims, Christians, Sikhs, Buddhists.

I'm not sure whether I am optimistic in the short term, but I am certainly more optimistic in the long term. Why? Because I see that the way refugees are being treated today is better than the Jews were treated in the 1930s. Then, all the doors were closed to us. Where could we go? I like the analogy of the smooth pebble that is washed up on the shore. How many thousands of years did it take for this pebble to become smooth and warm?

The world is getting better, but it takes a long time.

Epilogue

In 2002, I was asked to go back to Poland to make a documentary. I wavered because I wanted to go, but at the same time, I didn't want to. I hadn't been back there since the war. In the end, I did decide to go. The Rosh Hashanah before we left, the '45 Aid Society Journal came out, which I always read from cover to cover. I always want to know what is going on with "The Boys." In the journal, I read the story of a man named Jakub Gutenbaum who had been in Skarżysko and was liberated in Theresienstadt. He had gone back to Warsaw after the war to look for his father and uncle who had run away to the Soviet Union at the beginning of the war, like many people had. With great difficulty, he had found his uncle, but unfortunately his father had died in Siberia. Gutenbaum stayed in Poland after the war and studied there. He became a university professor and was well known. At one point, he had also been the chair of the Polish organization called Children of the Holocaust.

When I read his story, I decided that, since I was going to Poland for the first time and didn't know anybody, I would like to meet him. I telephoned the chair of the '45 Aid Society, whom I knew well, and asked him if he had any information about this man. He said he did, that he had been in Schlieben with him, and he gave me his phone number. I phoned this man, told him I had also been in Skarżysko, and that I wanted to meet him when I came to Warsaw.

When we arrived in Warsaw, I made arrangements for him to come and have tea with Dorothy and me at the hotel where we were staying. When he arrived, well-dressed, the first question he asked me was how I had survived the selection at Skarżysko, since few young people survived that day. I told him my story and how Katz had saved my life. When I finished telling him my story, I asked him how he had survived. He responded that he had been selected by Schulze to die and described how they were driven into a ring guarded by the SS and Ukrainians. They had machine guns and anyone who tried to run away was shot. Still, some people tried to run. While they were being held in this circle, Gutenbaum bit the hand of the nearest German or Ukrainian to him so hard that the guard let go, and in the mayhem he ran. They shot after him but he managed to hide until the next morning when he was sent to Schlieben with the rest of the survivors.

When Gutenbaum got up to say goodbye, I noticed that one of his shoes was built up by about five centimetres. I hadn't noticed that when he came in, nor had I noticed that he had a slight limp. Yaakov was the only child in Skarżysko Werk C who had a genetic fault. His right leg was shorter than his left and he had a limp. I started crying when I realized whom I had been talking to, and I still get tears in my eyes when I tell this story today.

When I told him who I was, though, it didn't mean anything to him. I pictured him in his rags, limping, and I remembered thinking that he had been murdered as a sacrificial lamb for me so it meant a great deal to me, but I don't think he even remembered that we had been such close friends. We kept in touch a little after that first meeting, although our friendship was never really rekindled. But I no longer had to mourn him.

Glossary

Aktion (German; pl. *Aktionen*) A brutal roundup of Jews for mass murder by shooting or for deportation to forced labour, concentration and death camps.

antisemitism Prejudice, discrimination, persecution or hatred against Jewish people, institutions, culture and symbols.

Appell (German; also *Zählappell*) Roll call. In Nazi camps, roll calls, the practice of gathering inmates to count who was present, were part of a series of daily humiliations for prisoners, who were often made to stand completely still for hours regardless of weather conditions.

Aryan A nineteenth-century anthropological term originally used to refer to the Indo-European family of languages and, by extension, the peoples who spoke them. It became a synonym for people of Nordic or Germanic descent in the theories that inspired Nazi racial ideology. "Aryan" was an official classification in Nazi racial laws to denote someone of pure Germanic blood, as opposed to "non-Aryans," such as Slavs, Jews, part-Jews, Roma and Sinti, and others of supposedly inferior racial stock.

bar mitzvah, bat mitzvah (Hebrew; literally, son/daughter of the commandment) The time when, in Jewish tradition, children become religiously and morally responsible for their actions and are considered adults for the purpose of synagogue and other rituals.

Traditionally this occurs at age thirteen for boys and twelve for girls. A bar mitzvah or bat mitzvah is also the synagogue ceremony and family celebration that marks the attainment of this status, during which the bar mitzvah boy — and in more liberal Jewish communities, the bat mitzvah girl — is called upon to read a portion of the Torah and recite the prescribed prayers in a public prayer service. Variations of this ceremony for girls are often held in Orthodox practice as well.

black market An illegal and informal economic system that arises, often in wartime, due to shortages or government control of goods.

Blockältester (German, male; block elder; pl. *Blockältesten*) A camp inmate appointed by the Nazi authorities to serve as barracks supervisor, charged with maintaining order and accorded certain privileges.

British Mandate Palestine (Also Mandatory Palestine) The area of the Middle East under British rule from 1923 to 1948 comprising present-day Israel, Jordan, the West Bank and the Gaza Strip. The Mandate was established by the League of Nations after World War I and the collapse of the Ottoman Empire; the area was given to the British to administer until a Jewish national home could be established. During this time, Jewish immigration was severely restricted, and Jews and Arabs clashed with the British and each other as they struggled to realize their national interests. The Mandate ended on May 15, 1948, after the United Nations Partition Plan for Palestine was adopted and on the same day that the State of Israel was declared.

Buchenwald A concentration camp complex located near Weimar, Germany, that was in operation between July 1937 and April 1945. Over the course of Buchenwald's existence, an estimated 240,000 prisoners passed through the camp from every country in Europe. The Buchenwald complex comprised at least ninety subcamps, which by 1944 held approximately 43,000 prisoners. Prisoners were used as forced labourers, and many were subject to medical

experimentation and extreme brutality. Because so many prisoners were never registered, the complete mortality rate is indeter-
minable; postwar documents and evidence from the camp point
to the deaths of at least 56,000 men. In the spring of 1945, many
of the prisoners were evacuated and sent on death marches; other
prisoners eventually took over the camp, right before Buchenwald
was liberated by the US army in April 1945.

cantor (in Hebrew, *chazzan*) A person who leads a synagogue congregation in songful prayer. The cantor might be professionally
trained or a member of the congregation.

Central British Fund (CBF) An organization whose full name was
the Central British Fund for German Jewry, established in 1933 to
aid Jews being persecuted in Germany. Starting in 1938, the CBF
helped to transport and rescue close to 10,000 German-Jewish
children via a relief effort called the Kindertransport and helped
settle the youth in Britain; in 1945, the CBF (then called the Central British Fund for Relief and Rehabilitation) brought 732 Jewish
orphans from Europe to Britain. The Central British Fund, now
known as World Jewish Relief, has continued to respond to hu-
manitarian crises since World War II. *See also* Goldsmid-Montefiore, Leonard.

challah (Hebrew) Braided egg bread traditionally eaten on the Jewish
Sabbath as well as on other Jewish holidays.

cheder (Hebrew; room) A traditional Jewish elementary school in
which religious studies and Hebrew are taught.

chevra kadisha (Aramaic; holy society) Jewish burial society. An
organization of Jewish volunteers who prepare a dead body for
burial according to Jewish tradition.

Children of the Holocaust A Polish association founded in 1991 to
offer community programming and support to child survivors of
the Holocaust. The organization's first meeting, chaired by survivor Jakub Gutenbaum (1929–2017) — a post he would hold for
nine years — was attended by forty-five survivors. Children of the

Holocaust currently has four branches in Poland, with a membership of six hundred survivors.

cholent (Yiddish) A traditional Jewish stew usually prepared on Friday and slow-cooked overnight to be eaten for Shabbat (the Sabbath) lunch. Ingredients for cholent vary by geographic region, but usually include meat, potatoes, beans and a grain.

chremzlach (Yiddish; also *chremzel, chremzli*) Fried pancakes made from matzah meal or potatoes, often eaten during the Jewish holidays of Passover and Chanukah. *See also* Passover.

cohen (Hebrew; pl. *cohanim*) In biblical times, the word for priest. The *cohanim* were responsible for worship ceremonies in the days of the Temple in Jerusalem. In the post-biblical era, a *cohen* refers to a male Jew who can trace his ancestry to the family of Judaism's first priest, Aaron, the brother of Moses. *Cohanim* occupy a special ritual status in Judaism (such as reciting certain blessings in synagogues). According to Jewish traditions, particular rules apply to a *cohen*, such as having no contact with dead bodies and not marrying a divorcee or a convert to Judaism.

Colditz A forced labour camp established in 1944 in the district of Leipzig, Germany, that was a subcamp of Buchenwald. In November 1944, the HASAG armaments factory opened a forced labour camp in Colditz on the site of a former porcelain factory. The camp was divided into a section for prisoners — holding 650 Jewish men at the height of its existence — and a section for the military plant, where Jewish forced labourers worked alongside Polish civilian forced labourers, who were held in separate barracks. The Colditz camp was dissolved on April 14, 1945, and its 650 prisoners were forced on a death march toward Theresienstadt along with 1,000 others from nearby camps. *See also* Buchenwald; HASAG; Theresienstadt.

Czerniaków, Adam (1880–1942) The first leader of the Judenrat in the Warsaw ghetto. On July 23, 1942, one day after the Nazis ordered that thousands of Warsaw's Jews be deported to the Treblinka killing centre, Czerniaków committed suicide. *See also* Judenrat.

Final Solution (in German: *Die Endlösung der Judenfrage*) An abbreviation of the euphemistic term the "Final Solution to the Jewish Question," the Nazi plan for the systematic murder of Europe's Jewish population between 1941 and 1945.

Gerrer Rebbe The spiritual head of a Hasidic group originating in Góra Kalwaria, near Warsaw, Poland. During World War II, Avraham Mordechai Alter (1866–1948) was Gerrer Rebbe, the third to hold this position. He escaped Warsaw and arrived in Jerusalem in 1940, establishing a Hasidic centre there, which today is headed by one of his grandsons.

Gestapo (German; abbreviation of Geheime Staatspolizei, the Secret State Police) The Nazi regime's brutal political police that operated without legal constraints to deal with its perceived enemies. The Gestapo was formed in 1933 under Hermann Göring; it was taken over by Heinrich Himmler in 1934 and became a department within the SS in 1939. During the Holocaust, the Gestapo set up offices in Nazi-occupied countries and was responsible for rounding up Jews and sending them to concentration and death camps. They also arrested, tortured and deported those who resisted Nazi policies. A number of Gestapo members also belonged to the Einsatzgruppen, the mobile killing squads responsible for mass shooting operations of Jews in the Soviet Union.

ghetto A confined residential area for Jews. The term originated in Venice, Italy, in 1516 with a law requiring all Jews to live on a segregated, gated island known as Ghetto Nuovo. Throughout the Middle Ages in Europe, Jews were often forcibly confined to gated Jewish neighbourhoods. Beginning in 1939, the Nazis forced Jews to live in crowded and unsanitary conditions in designated areas — usually the poorest ones — of cities and towns in Eastern Europe. Ghettos were often enclosed by walls and gates, and entry and exit from the ghettos were strictly controlled. Family and community life continued to some degree, but starvation and disease were rampant. Starting in 1941, the ghettos were liquidated, and Jews were deported to camps and killing centres. *See also* "Jewish Gestapo"; Warsaw ghetto; Warsaw Ghetto Uprising.

Goldsmid-Montefiore, Leonard (1889–1961) A British philanthropist involved in numerous and varied organizations to help Jewish citizens and refugees. In 1926, Goldsmid-Montefiore became president of the Anglo-Jewish Association; he was also involved with the Jewish Board of Guardians, the Jewish Association for the Protection of Girls and Women, the Bernhard Baron Settlement, the Council of the Jewish Colonization Association and the Central British Fund for German Jewry. *See also* Central British Fund.

Gymnasium (German) A word used throughout Central and Eastern Europe to mean high school or secondary school.

Harvest Festival (also called Operation Harvest Festival) The code name for the German plan to murder all remaining Jews in the Lublin region of occupied Poland in response to the increasing instances of Jewish prisoner uprisings in camps and ghettos. From November 3-4, 1943, the SS and police massacred about 42,000 Jewish prisoners in Majdanek and the Poniatowa and Trawniki forced labour camps; in Majdanek and Trawniki, music was played through loudspeakers to mask the sound of the murders. Jews hiding outside the camps were captured by local collaborators and killed during the operation. *See also* Majdanek.

HASAG (acronym for Hugo Schneider Aktiengesellschaft Metallwarenfabrik) A small lamp factory company that originated in Leipzig, Germany, in 1863, which grew to become a metal products factory in 1889. HASAG began supplying munitions to the German military in 1933; by 1934 it earned the official status of a military plant and in 1939 it was classified as an armaments company. HASAG, the third-largest private company to use concentration camp prisoners as forced labour during the war, established six forced labour camps in Poland. In 1944, seven forced labour camps, subcamps of Buchenwald, were established by HASAG in Germany. Approximately 41,000 prisoners passed through the HASAG camps; the number of survivors is unknown. In 1948, twenty-five HASAG managers were tried for war crimes in Leipzig, Germany — four were sentenced to death; two were given life sentences; and eighteen were sentenced to prison terms ranging from one to five years. *See also* Buchenwald; Colditz; Skarżysko-Kamienna.

Hasidic Judaism (also Hasidism, Hasidim; from the Hebrew word *hasid*; pious person) An Orthodox Jewish spiritual movement founded by Rabbi Israel ben Eliezer (1698–1760), better known as the Baal Shem Tov, in eighteenth-century Poland. The Hasidic movement, characterized by philosophies of mysticism and focusing on joyful prayer, resulted in a new kind of leader who attracted disciples as opposed to the traditional rabbis who focused on the intellectual study of Jewish law.

High Holidays (also High Holy Days) The period of time leading up to and including the Jewish autumn holidays of Rosh Hashanah (New Year) and Yom Kippur (Day of Atonement) that is considered a time for introspection and renewal. Rosh Hashanah is observed with synagogue services, the blowing of the shofar (ram's horn) and festive meals during which sweet foods, such as apples and honey, are eaten to symbolize and celebrate a sweet new year. Yom Kippur, a day of fasting and prayer, occurs ten days after Rosh Hashanah.

"Jewish Gestapo" (also known as the "Thirteen"; in Polish, *trzynastka*) A Jewish faction of the German Security Police whose name — the "Thirteen" — came from the address of their headquarters on Leszno Street. Founded in the fall of 1940 and comprising between three hundred and four hundred uniformed Jewish officers, the unit's official function was to oversee the Office to Combat Usury and Profiteering in the Jewish Quarter of Warsaw; in reality, the collaborationist force primarily engaged in self-serving blackmail of ghetto residents. The force was disbanded in June or July 1941 and many of its members were eventually murdered by the Nazis.

Jewish ghetto police (in German, Ordnungsdienst; Order Service) The police force that reported to the Jewish Councils, under Nazi order. The Jewish ghetto police were armed with clubs and carried out various tasks in the ghettos, such as traffic control and guarding the ghetto gates. Eventually, some policemen also participated in rounding up Jews for forced labour and transportation to the death camps, carrying out the orders of the Nazis. There has been much debate and controversy surrounding the role of both the Jewish Councils and the Jewish police. Even though the Jewish police exercised considerable power within the ghetto, to the Nazis these policemen were still Jews and subject to the same fate as other Jews. *See also* Judenrat.

Judenrat (German; pl. Judenräte; Jewish Council) A group of Jewish leaders appointed by the German occupiers to administer the ghettos and carry out Nazi orders. The Judenräte tried to provide social services to the Jewish population to alleviate the harsh conditions of the ghettos and maintain a sense of community. Although the Judenräte appeared to be self-governing entities, they were actually under complete Nazi control. The Judenräte faced difficult and complex moral decisions under brutal conditions — they had to decide whether to cooperate with or resist Nazi demands, when refusal likely meant death, and they had to determine which actions might save some of the population and which might worsen their fates. The Judenräte were under extreme pressure and they remain a contentious subject.

Kaddish (Aramaic; holy. Also known as the Mourner's Kaddish or Mourner's Prayer.) The prayer recited by mourners at funerals and memorials and during Jewish prayer services. Kaddish is traditionally said by a relative of the deceased for eleven months after the death of a parent and for thirty days after the death of a spouse or sibling, as well as each year on the anniversary of the death.

kapo (German) A concentration camp prisoner appointed by the SS to supervise other prisoners in exchange for special privileges, like extra food or better sleeping arrangements. The kapos were often cruel to their fellow prisoners.

Kiddush (Hebrew; sanctification) The blessing over wine that is recited on Shabbat and other Jewish holidays. *See also* Shabbos.

korban (Hebrew; sacrifice) A sacrifice brought to the Temple in Jerusalem.

Lagerältester (German, male; camp elder) A camp inmate appointed by the Nazi authorities to be in charge of the entire prisoner population and who reported directly to the SS.

Majdanek A multipurpose Nazi camp in Lublin, Poland, that opened when its construction began in October 1941. People from twenty-eight countries were incarcerated at Majdanek, with Jews and Poles being the largest groups. Between the fall of 1942 and late 1943, mass murder operations by poison gas were in effect in the camp. Both a death camp and a concentration camp, Majdanek served different functions at various points of its existence — it used prisoners for forced labour; it held suspected Polish insurgents; it operated as a transit camp; and it acted as a storage centre for personal belongings taken from Jews before their deaths in other death camps. Tens of thousands of Jewish prisoners were killed at the camp. Majdanek was liberated by the Soviet army in July 1944, although fewer than 500 prisoners remained in what was then merely a remnant of the operational camp.

minyan (Hebrew; count, number) The quorum of ten adult Jews required for certain religious rites. The term can also designate a congregation.

National Party The governing party of South Africa between 1948 and 1994, when the party was dissolved and rebranded under the name of the New National Party. The New National Party was disbanded in 2005, after failing to distance itself from the policies of the National Party, foremost of which was apartheid, racial segregation.

Oneg Shabbat (Hebrew; Joy of Sabbath) A clandestine organization and archive founded by historian Emanuel Ringelblum to document the ongoing strife, daily life and persecution in the Warsaw ghetto. The group gathered on Shabbat on Saturdays, hence its name, and wrote and collected testimonies, newspapers and other evidence of their ongoing existence and the Nazis' persecution and deportation of the Jews. Members buried the collection of materials in a number of large milk jugs and metal containers, two of which were discovered after the war. The more than 25,000 pages that were recovered are held at the Jewish Historical Institute in Warsaw. *See also* Ringelblum, Emanuel.

Organization for Rehabilitation through Training (ORT) A vocational school system founded for Jews by Jews in Russia in 1880 to promote economic self-sufficiency in impoverished communities. The name ORT derives from the acronym of the Russian organization Obshestvo Remeslenogo Zemledelcheskogo Truda, Society for Trades and Agricultural Labour. ORT schools continued to operate through World War II. After the war, ORT set up rehabilitation programs for the survivors, serving approximately 85,000 people in 78 DP camps in Germany. Today, ORT is a nonprofit organization that provides educational services to communities all over the world.

Passover (in Hebrew, Pesach) An eight-day Jewish festival that takes place in the spring and commemorates the exodus of the Israelite slaves from Egypt. The festival begins with a lavish ritual meal called a seder, during which the story of the Exodus is told through the reading of a Jewish text called the Haggadah. During Passover, Jews refrain from eating any leavened foods. The name of the festival refers to God's "passing over" the houses of the Jews and sparing their lives during the last of the ten plagues, when the first-born sons of Egyptians were killed by God. *See also* seder.

peyes (Yiddish; in Hebrew, *peyote*; sidelocks.) Among certain Orthodox Jewish communities, males refrain from cutting the hair at the edge of the face, in front of the ears. The practice of growing these distinctive locks of hair is based on a strict interpretation of the biblical verse "You shall not round off the side-growth of your head, or destroy the side-growth of your beard" (Lev. 19:27).

picrid acid (from Greek word *pikros*; bitter) An organic compound first commonly used as an explosive in the late nineteenth century.

post-traumatic stress disorder (PTSD) A condition that results from experiencing an extremely traumatic event. PTSD was first classified as an anxiety disorder in 1980; the definition has since been revised and it is now considered a Trauma- and Stressor-Related Disorder. Symptoms of PTSD include recurring nightmares of the event as well as daytime thoughts and images that can result in panic, dread or fear.

Rashi (1040–1105) The acronym for Rabbi Shlomo Yitzhaki, a French-born rabbi who wrote the most widely studied commentary on the Torah (Hebrew bible) and the Talmud. *See also* Talmud.

Ringelblum, Emanuel (1900–1944) The historian, educator, relief worker and writer who is most known for his diligence and leadership in archiving testimonies and other material evidence from the Warsaw ghetto. Ringelblum escaped from the ghetto in March 1943 but returned the next month, on the eve of the Warsaw Ghetto Uprising. He was eventually deported to the Trawniki labour camp, from where he was smuggled out, and was in hiding in Warsaw. Ringelblum was caught by the Nazis in the spring of 1944 and was murdered in the remnants of the Warsaw ghetto. *See also* Oneg Shabbat.

seder (Hebrew; order) A ritual meal celebrated at the beginning of the festival of Passover. A traditional seder involves reading the Haggadah, which tells the story of the Israelite slaves' exodus from Egypt; drinking four cups of wine; eating matzah and other symbolic foods which are arranged on a special seder plate; partaking in a festive meal; and singing traditional songs.

Shabbos (Yiddish; Sabbath) The weekly day of rest beginning Friday at sunset and ending Saturday at nightfall, ushered in by the lighting of candles on Friday evening and the recitation of blessings over wine and challah (egg bread). A day of celebration as well as prayer, it is customary to eat three festive meals, attend synagogue services and refrain from doing any work or travelling.

sheitel (Yiddish) A wig that is worn by some Jewish women to abide by the traditional Orthodox requirement for married women to cover their hair.

shtiebl (Yiddish; pl. *shtieblach*; little house or little room) A small informal space used for prayer and study, often in a house or storefront. Most observant Jews in Eastern Europe prayed in *shtieblach* on a daily basis, and there are still *shtieblach* in Jewish communities throughout the world.

Sinai War Also known as the Suez Crisis. The conflict between Israel, Britain and France against Egypt in October 1956 after Egypt's President Nasser seized control of the Suez Canal. Israel, who wanted to secure its southern border, invaded the Sinai Peninsula backed by France and Britain, who wanted to maintain control over the canal as a vital waterway. The conflict ended with the withdrawal of troops from the Sinai Peninsula in March 1957 because of international pressure, and a United Nations peacekeeping force was placed in the area.

Skarżysko-Kamienna The site of a HASAG munitions plant in June 1940 that became a forced labour camp near the town of the same name in Poland in 1942. The Skarżysko-Kamienna camp was divided into three work camps and used both Polish civilian labour and Jewish forced labourers. Between 1942 and 1943, 17,000 prisoners passed through the camp, 6,500 of whom had survived by the time the camp was dissolved on August 1, 1944. *See also* HASAG.

tallis (Yiddish; pl. *taleisim*; prayer shawl) A four-cornered ritual garment traditionally worn during morning prayers and on the Day of Atonement (Yom Kippur). Fringes on the four corners of the garment are meant to remind the wearer to fulfill the biblical commandments.

Talmud (Hebrew; study) A collection of ancient rabbinic teachings compiled between the third and sixth centuries that includes explications of scriptural law in a text known as the Mishnah and deliberations about the Mishnah in a text known as the Gemara. The Talmud remains a focus of Jewish study and the basis of traditional Jewish law and practice today. *See also* Torah.

tefillin (Hebrew; phylacteries) A pair of black leather boxes containing scrolls of parchment inscribed with Bible verses and worn by Jews on the arm and forehead at prescribed times of prayer as a symbol of the covenantal relationship with God.

Theresienstadt (German; in Czech, Terezín) A walled town in the Czech Republic sixty kilometres north of Prague that served as a ghetto, a transit camp and a concentration camp. Many of the Jews sent to Theresienstadt had been exempted from deportation to the east either because they were elderly, or they were decorated or disabled veterans of the German army, or they were considered prominent. Despite the terrible living conditions in the ghetto, a rich cultural life developed that included artistic performances, clandestine schools and a vast lending library. The Nazis showcased Theresienstadt as a model ghetto for propaganda purposes, to demonstrate to delegates from the International Red Cross and others their supposedly humane treatment of Jews and to counter information reaching the Allies about Nazi atrocities and mass murder. In total, approximately 140,000 Jews were deported to Theresienstadt between 1941 and 1945. About 33,000 prisoners died in Theresienstadt, and nearly 90,000 others were sent on to death camps, including Auschwitz-Birkenau. The Soviet army liberated the remaining prisoners on May 9, 1945.

Tisha B'Av (Hebrew; the ninth day of Av) A day of fasting that commemorates the destructions of the First and Second Temples in Jerusalem — in 586 BCE and 70 CE, respectively.

Torah (Hebrew; instruction) The first five books of the Hebrew Bible, also known as the Five Books of Moses or Chumash, the content of which is traditionally believed to have been revealed to Moses on Mount Sinai; or, the entire canon of the twenty-four books of the Hebrew Bible, referred to as the Old Testament in Christianity. Torah is also broadly used to refer to all the teachings that were given to the Jewish people through divine revelation or even through rabbinic writings (called the Oral Torah).

ulpan (Hebrew; pl. *ulpanim*) An intensive Hebrew-language study program for new immigrants to Israel, first established in Jerusalem in 1949. *Ulpanim* also teach Israeli culture, history and geography to help new immigrants acclimatize to life in Israel.

Umschlagplatz (German) A collection point, used to refer to the areas where the Nazis assembled Jews for deportation to death camps. The term is most often used in connection to the Warsaw ghetto.

United Nations Relief and Rehabilitation Administration (UNRRA) An international relief agency created at a 44-nation conference in Washington, DC, on November 9, 1943, to provide economic assistance and basic necessities to war refugees. It was especially active in repatriating and assisting refugees in the formerly Nazi-occupied European nations immediately after World War II.

Volksdeutsche (German; German-folk) The term used by the Nazis to refer to the ethnic Germans living outside Germany, mostly in Eastern Europe. Nazis estimated that there were 30 million *Volksdeutsche* and used them to support their idea of a pure-blooded German race and to further their plans to expand to the east. *Volksdeutsche* were given special status and benefits, such as property that had been stolen from Jews and Poles, and many saw the Nazis as liberators. After the collapse of Nazi Germany, most *Volksdeutsche* were expelled to Germany.

Warsaw ghetto A small area in the city of Warsaw where approximately 400,000 Jews were forced to live beginning in October 1940. Enclosed by a ten-foot wall, the ghetto's horrific conditions led to the death of 83,000 people from starvation and disease. Mass deportations from the ghetto to the Treblinka killing centre were carried out between July and September 1942. See also *Umschlagplatz*; Warsaw Ghetto Uprising.

Warsaw Ghetto Uprising A large rebellion by Jewish resistance fighters in the Warsaw ghetto, beginning on April 19, 1943, and lasting several weeks. After the mass deportation and murder of ghetto inhabitants in the summer of 1942, resistance groups prepared for an uprising. In January 1943, the Nazis attempted to deport the remaining Jews, but they encountered armed resistance and suspended deportations. When the Nazis entered the ghetto to deport the remaining inhabitants in April 1943, about 750 organized ghetto fighters launched an insurrection, while the other inhabitants took shelter in hiding places and underground bunkers. The resistance fighters were defeated on May 16, 1943, resulting in the destruction of the ghetto and the deportation of the remaining Jews; more than 56,000 Jews were captured and deported, and about 7,000 were shot.

Warthegau (Wartheland) The area of western-occupied Poland that was incorporated into Greater Germany in October 1939. Under Nazi control, Warthegau was slated to become completely "Germanized," meaning that citizens of an "inferior" race — mostly Jews, as well as Poles and Roma — were to be severely persecuted and Germans were to colonize the area. In Warthegau, 173 ghettos and labour camps were created; by the end of the war, 380,000 Jews who had lived in Warthegau had been murdered.

yahrzeit (Yiddish) The anniversary of a death as it occurs on the Jewish calendar, often commemorated by reciting Kaddish and lighting a candle. *See also* Kaddish.

Photographs

The Wilker Synagogue on Zachodnia 56, Lodz, Poland. The synagogue was two buildings away from where Pinchas was born, on Zachodnia 54. Both buildings no longer exist. The synagogue, built between 1875 and 1878, was destroyed by the Nazis in 1940. (Photo credit: Synagoga Wilker Shul w Łodzi, Wikimedia Commons.)

Pinchas's aunt Sabina Shpiegelglas, who the Gutter family stayed with in Warsaw after fleeing from Lodz. Circa 1920.

Celebration of the wedding of Pinchas's cousin Michael to Terenya Levinson. In the back row, far left, is Uncle Moishe Shlome Levinson, Terenya's father; third from the left is Libel Lipsker, Pinchas's father's nephew; and fifth from the left is Rav Krol. Pinchas's cousin Michael, whom he saw in Skarżysko-Kamienna, is in the front row, third from the left. Lodz, 1938.

1 & 2 Copies of the first two pages of Pinchas's *Häftlings-Personal-Karte* from Buchenwald that was issued on January 20, 1945. The card states that Pinchas had been arrested for being a *Politische-Pole-Jude*, a political Polish Jew.

P. - Jude

Konzentrationslager _____ Art der Haft: _____ Gef.-Nr.: 115 800

Name und Vorname: Gutter Pinkus
geb.: 21. 7. 1927 zu: Litzmannstadt
Wohnort: Litzmannstadt ul. Zachodnia 54, Warthegau
Beruf: Arbeiter _____ Rel.: mos.
Staatsangehörigkeit: Pole _____ Stand: ledig
Name der Eltern: Vater: Schuster, Mendel G. z.Z. Rasse
Wohnort: Mutter: Ruchla, geb. Silberstein in Haft
Name der Ehefrau: _____ Rasse:
Wohnort: keine Ang
Kinder: _____ Alleiniger Ernährer der Familie oder der Eltern: 20.1.45 RSHA
Vorbildung:
Militärdienstzeit: _____ von — bis
Kriegsdienstzeit: Pinkus Gutter _____ von — bis
Grösse: _____ Nase: _____ Haare: _____ Gestalt:
Mund: _____ Bart: _____ Gesicht: _____ Ohren: 42 700
Sprache: _____ Augen: _____ Zähne:

1

P. Jude _____ 4352 115800

Vor- und Zuname: Pinkus Gutter _____ Haft-Nr.

Beruf: Arbeiter _____ geboren am: 21. 7. 27 _____ in: Litzmannstadt

Anschrifts-Ort: _____ Straße Nr.

Eingel. am: 20.1.45 Uhr von RSHA. _____ Entl. am _____ / _____ Uhr nach

Bei Einlieferung abgegeben:

				Koffer	Aktentasche	Paket
Hut/Mütze	Paar Schuhe/Stiefel	Kragenknöpfe		Feuerzeug		Wehrpaß
Mantel	Paar Strümpfe	Halstuch		Tabak	Pfeife	Fremdenpaß
Rock / Jacke	Paar Gamaschen	Taschentuch		Zigarren/Zigaretten		Arbeitsbuch
Weste/Kletterweste	Kragen	Paar Handschube Leder		Stg.-Blättchen		Invalidenkarte
Hose	Vorhemd	Brieftasche mit		Ziertuch		
Pullover	Binder/Fliege	Papiere		Messer / Schere		
Hosenträger	Paar Armelhalter	Sporthemd/Hosen		Bleistift/Drehblei		
Unterhemden	Paar Sockenhalter	Abzeichen		Geldbörse		
Unterhosen	Paar Mansch.-Knöpfe	Schlüssel a. Ring		Kamm		Wertsachen: ja—nein

Abgabe bestätigt: _____ Effektenverwalter:

Guter Pinek

2

1 & 2-Pages three and four of the _Häftlings-Personal-Karte._ As on the first document, the top image shows Pinchas's date of birth as 1927, which was, on the advice of his father, the false date he gave to the Nazis; stating that he was five years older than he really was helped him to pass selections. January 1945.

Pinchas at around age fourteen, wearing his new suit after the war. Ascot, England, 1946.

1

2

1 Pinchas (back row, second from left) with the Diamond family, whom he boarded with in London. In the back row, left to right: Keith Friedman, one of the Diamonds' sons-in-law; Pinchas; Uncle Izzie; and the Diamonds' other son-in-law. In front, left to right: the Diamonds' son, David; Mrs. Diamond; Mr. Diamond; and their daughters, Helen and Golda. London, circa 1947.

2 Pinchas (left) with Holocaust survivor friends in England, 1947.

1 Pinchas (standing, left), with cousins Rav Abraham Krol (seated, holding plate) and his wife, Andja Krol. Paris, 1949.

2 The Krol family. In front, left to right: Rav Krol's sister, Regina; Andja; and Rav Krol. In back, the Krols' daughter, Therese. France, circa 1949.

3 Pinchas with his new car. Paris, 1950.

1

2

1 Pinchas (left), with a friend on the SS *Negba* on his way to Israel to volunteer for the army. December, 1951.

2 Pinchas driving a Jeep in the army. Herzliya, Israel, 1952.

1

2

1 Pinchas (far right) at an officers' party. Israel, 1953.
2 Pinchas in Israel, 1954.

1

2

1 Dorothy (née Gelcer) and Pinchas Gutter on their wedding day. London,
   January 6, 1957.
2 Dorothy and Pinchas's wedding photo. London, January 6, 1957.

Pinchas serving as cantor at the Kiever Synagogue in Kensington Market.
Toronto, 1987. The congregation was established in 1912. Pinchas continues to act
as full-time honorary cantor to this day.

1 Pinchas receiving the President's Award from Alan Judelman for his charitable work at the Baycrest Centre for Geriatric Care. Toronto, 1989.

2 Pinchas, serving as chaplain, conducting a Passover seder at the Queen Elizabeth Hospital, a long-term care facility. Toronto, early 2000s.

Pinchas and Dorothy. Toronto, 1989.

The Gutter family at Majdanek during the filming of Stephen Smith's documentary *The Void: In Search of Memory Lost*. From left to right: Pinchas's daughter-in-law, Lauren, his son, Jan, Pinchas, Dorothy, and their daughters, Rumi and Tanya. 2002.

Pinchas and Dorothy with family at a tribute called "Treasures of Baycrest" to honour benefactors and those who volunteered their time to help the elderly community. Back row (left to right): Pinchas's daughter-in-law, Lauren; his grandson Daniel; his son, Jan; his grandson Adam; and his daughter Rumi. In front, Pinchas and Dorothy. Toronto, 2004.

Pinchas's granddaughter, Lara. Toronto, 2017.

1

2

3

1 Pinchas speaking to participants of the Sarah and Chaim Neuberger Holocaust Education Centre Holocaust Educator Study Tour at the former site of the Warsaw ghetto. Warsaw, July 2016.

2 Pinchas at the Warsaw Ghetto Wall during the Holocaust Educator Study Tour. Warsaw, 2016.

3 Holocaust Educator Study Tour. Warsaw, 2016.

Poster presented to Pinchas in honour of his participation in the March of Remembrance and Hope in 2015, signed by student participants.

Index

The Azrieli Foundation was established in 1989 to realize and extend the philanthropic vision of David J. Azrieli, C.M., C.Q., M.Arch. The Foundation's mission is to support a wide spectrum of initiatives in education and research. The Azrieli Foundation is an active supporter of programs in the fields of education, the education of architects, scientific and medical research, and the arts. The Azrieli Foundation's many initiatives include: the Holocaust Survivor Memoirs Program, which collects, preserves, publishes and distributes the written memoirs of survivors in Canada; the Azrieli Institute for Educational Empowerment, an innovative program successfully working to keep at-risk youth in school; the Azrieli Fellows Program, which promotes academic excellence and leadership on the graduate level at Israeli universities; the Azrieli Music Project, which celebrates and fosters the creation of high-quality new Jewish orchestral music; and the Azrieli Neurodevelopmental Research Program, which supports advanced research on neurodevelopmental disorders, particularly Fragile X and Autism Spectrum Disorders.